THE

WORDS OF JESUS.

BY THE AUTHOR OF

"THE MORNING AND NIGHT WATCHES," "THE FAITHFUL PROMISER," ETC.

Taken from the last London Edition.

New York:
STANFORD & DELISSER,
No. 508, BROADWAY.
1858.

The Words of Jesus.

"A WORD spoken in season," says the wise man, "how good it is!" If this be true regarding the utterances of uninspired lips, with what devout and paramount interest must we invest the sayings of Incarnate Truth—"the WORDS OF JESUS!"

We have, in the motto-verses which head the succeeding pages a few comforting responses from the Oracle of heavenly Wisdom—a few grapes plucked from the true Vine—living streams welling fresh from the Living Fountain. Every portion of Scripture is designed for nutriment to the soul—"the bread of life;" but surely we may well regard the recorded "*Words of Jesus*" as "the finest of the wheat". These are the "Honey" out of the true "Rock," with which He will "satisfy" us. "The WORDS that I speak unto you, they are spirit and they are life."

The following are selected more especially as "*Words for the Weary*"—healing leaves for the wounded spirit falling from the Tree of Life. Jesus was divinely qualified for this special office of speaking "many and *comfortable* words." "The Lord God hath given me the tongue of the learned, that I might know how to speak a *Word in Season* to him that is *weary*."

Let us, like the disciple of Patmos, turn to hear the voice that speaks to us, saying, "I wait for the Lord, my soul doth wait, and in *His Word* do I hope." Eighteen hundred years have elapsed since these "words" were uttered. With tones of unaltered and unchanged affection, they are still echoed from the inner sanctuary—they come this day fresh as they were spoken, from the lips of Him whose memorial to all time is this: "*that same Jesus*."

Reader, seek to realise, in meditating on them, the simple but solemn truth—"*Christ speaks to me!*" Surely nothing can be more soothing with which to close your eyes on your nightly pillow, or to carry with you in the morning out to the duties (or, it may be, the trials and sorrows) of the day, than—"A WORD OF JESUS."

1ST DAY OF MONTH.

"Remember the words of the Lord Jesus, how He said"—

"Come unto me all ye that labour and are heavy laden, and I will give you rest."—Matt. xi. 28.

The Gracious Invitation.

GRACIOUS "word" of a gracious Saviour, on which the soul may confidingly repose, and be at peace for ever? It is a *present* rest—the rest of *grace* as well as the rest of *glory*. Not only are there signals of peace hung out from the walls of heaven—the lights of Home glimmering in the distance to cheer our footsteps; but we have the "shadow" of this "great Rock" in a *present* "weary land." Before the Throne alone is there "the sea of glass," without one rippling wave; but there is a haven even on earth for the tempest-tossed—"We which have believed DO enter into rest."

Reader, hast thou found this blessed

repose in the blood and work of Immanuel? Long going about "seeking rest and finding none," does this "word" sound like music in thine ears—"*Come unto Me?*" All other peace is counterfeit, shadowy, unreal. The eagle spurns the gilded cage as a poor equivalent for his free-born soarings. The soul's immortal aspirations can be satisfied with nothing short of the possession of God's favour and love in Jesus.

How unqualified is the invitation! If there had been one condition in entering this covenant Ark, we must have been through eternity at the mercy of the storm. But all are alike warranted and welcome, and none *more* warranted than welcome. For the weak, the weary, the sin-burdened and sorrow-burdened, there is an open door of grace.

Return, then unto thy rest, O my soul! Let the sweet cadence of this "word of Jesus" steal on thee amid the disquietudes of earth. Sheltered in Him, thou art safe for time, safe for eternity! There may be, and *will* be, temporary tossings, fears, and misgivings,—manifestations of inward corruption; but these will only be like the surface-heavings of the ocean, while underneath there is a deep settled calm. "Thou wilt keep him in perfect peace" (*lit.* peace, peace)"whose mind is stayed on Thee." In the world it is care on care, trouble on trouble, sin on sin; but every wave that breaks on the believer's soul seems sweetly to murmur, "Peace, peace!"

And if the foretaste of this rest be precious, what must be the glorious consummation? Awaking in the morning of immortality, with the unquiet dream of earth over—faith lost in sight, and hope in fruition;—no more any bias to sin—no more latent principles of evil—nothing to disturb the spirit's deep, everlasting tranquillity—the trembling magnet of the heart reposing, where alone it can confidingly and permanently rest, in the enjoyment of the Infinite God.

"THESE THINGS HAVE I SPOKEN UNTO YOU, THAT IN ME YE MIGHT HAVE PEACE."

2D DAY.

"Remember the words of the Lord Jesus, how He said"—

"Your heavenly Father knoweth that ye have need of al these things."—Matt. vi. 32.

The Comforting Assurance.

THOUGH spoken originally by Jesus regarding temporal things, this may be taken as a motto for the child of God amid all the changing vicissitudes of his changing history. How it should lull all misgivings; silence all murmurings; lead to lowly, unquestioning submissiveness —"My Heavenly Father knoweth that I have need of all these things."

Where can a child be safer or better than in a father's hand? Where can the believer be better than in the hands of his God? We are poor judges of what is best. We are under safe guidance with infallible wisdom. If we are tempted in a moment of rash presumption to say, "All these things are against me," let this "word" rebuke the hasty and unworthy surmise. Unerring wisdom and Fatherly love have pronounced *all* to be "needful."

My soul, is there aught that is disturbing thy peace? Are providences dark, or crosses heavy? Are spiritual props removed, creature comforts curtailed, gourds smitten and withered like grass?—write on each, "*Your Father knoweth that ye have need of all these things.*" It was He who increased thy burden. Why? "*It was needed.*" It was He who smote down thy clay idol. Why? "*It was needed.*" It was supplanting Himself: He had to remove it! It was He who crossed thy worldly schemes, marred thy cherished hopes. Why? "*It was needed.*" There was a lurking thorn in the coveted path. There was some higher spiritual blessing in reversion. "He '*prevented*' thee with the blessings of His goodness"

Seek to cherish a spirit of more childlike confidence in thy Heavenly Father's will. Thou art not left unbefriended and alone to buffet the storms of the wilderness. Thy Marahs as well as thy Elims are appointed by Him. A gracious pillar-cloud is before thee. Follow it through sunshine and storm. He may "lead thee about," but He will not lead thee wrong. Unutterable tenderness is the characteristic of all His dealings. "Blessed be His name," says a tried believer, "He maketh my feet like hinds' feet" (*literally*, "equaleth" them), "he *equaleth* them for every precipice, every ascent, every leap."

And who is it that speaks this quieting word? It is He who Himself felt the preciousness of the assurance during His own awful sufferings, that all were *needed*, and all *appointed;* that from Bethlehem's cradle to Calvary's Cross there was not the redundant thorn in the chaplet of sorrow which

He, the Man of Sorrows, bore. Every drop in His bitter cup was mingled by His Father: "This cup which *Thou* givest me to drink, shall I not drink it!" Oh, if He could extract comfort in this hour of inconceivable agony, in the thought that a Father's hand lighted the fearful furnace-fires, what strong consolation is there in the same truth to all His suffering people!

What! one superfluous drop! one redundant pang! one unneeded cross! Hush the secret atheism! He gave His Son for thee! He calls Himself "thy Father!" Whatever be the trial under which thou art now smarting, let the word of a gracious Saviour be "like oil thrown on the fretful sea;" let it dry every rebellious tear-drop. "He, thine unerring Parent, knoweth that thou hast need of *this* as well as *all* these things."

"THY WORD IS VERY SURE, THEREFORE THY SERVANT LOVETH IT."

3D DAY.

"Remember the words of the Lord Jesus, how He said"—

"Whatsoever ye shall ask in my name, that will I do, that the Father may be glorified in the Son."—John xiv. 13.

The Power of Prayer.

BLESSED JESUS! it is Thou who hast unlocked to Thy people the gates of prayer. Without Thee they must have been shut forever. It was Thy atoning merit on earth that first opened them; it is Thy intercessory work in heaven that keeps them open still.

How unlimited the promise—"*Whatsoever ye shall ask!*" It is the pledge of all that the needy sinner requires—all that an Omnipotent Saviour can bestow! As the great Steward of the mysteries of grace, He seems to say to His faithful servants, "Take thy bill, and under this, my superscription, write what you please." And then, when the blank is filled up, he further endorses each petition with the words, "*I* WILL *do it!*"

He farther encourages us to ask "*in His name.*" In the case of an earthly petitioner there are some pleas more influential in obtaining a boon than others. Jesus speaks of *this* as forming the key to the heart of God. As David loved the helpless cripple of Saul's house "*for Jonathan's sake,*" so will the Father, by virtue of our covenant relationship to the true JONATHAN (*lit.*, "the gift of God"), delight in giving us even "exceeding abundantly above all that we can ask or think."

Reader, do you know the blessedness of confiding your every want and every care—your every sorrow and every cross—into the ear of the Saviour? He is the "Wonderful Counsellor." With an exquisitely tender sympathy He can enter into the innermost depths of your need. That need may be great, but the everlasting arms are underneath it all. Think of Him now, at this moment—the great Angel of the Covenant, with the censer full of much incense, in which are placed your feeblest aspirations, your most burdened sighs—the odour-breathing cloud ascending with acceptance before the Father's throne. The answer may tarry;—these your supplications may seem to be kept long on the wing, hovering around the mercy-seat. A gracious God sometimes sees it meet thus to test the faith and patience of His people. He delights to hear the music of their importunate pleadings—to see them undeterred by difficulties—unrepelled by apparent forgetfulness and neglect. But He *will* come at last; the pent-up fountain of love and mercy will at length burst out;—the soothing accents will in His own good time be heard, "Be it unto thee according to thy word!"

Soldier of Christ! with all thine other panoply, forget not the "*All-*

prayer." It is that which keeps bright and shining "the whole armour of God." While yet out in the night of a dark world—whilst still bivouacking in an enemy's country—kindle thy watch-fires at the altar of incense. Thou must be Moses, pleading on the Mount, if thou wouldst be Joshua, victorious in the world's daily battle. Confide thy cause to this waiting Redeemer. Thou canst not weary Him with thine importunity. He delights in hearing. His Father is glorified in giving. The memorable Bethany-utterance remains unaltered and unrepealed—"I knew that Thou hearest me always." He is still the "Prince that has power with God and prevails"—still He promises and pleads—still He lives and loves!

"I WAIT FOR THE LORD, MY SOUL DOTH WAIT; AND IN HIS WORD DO I HOPE."

4TH DAY.

"Remember the words of the Lord Jesus, how He said"—

"What I do thou knowest not now; but thou shalt know hereafter."—John xiii. 7.

The Unveiled Dealings.

O BLESSED day, when the long sealed book of mystery shall be unfolded, when the "fountains of the great deep shall be broken up," "the channels of the waters seen," and *all* discovered to be one vast revelation of unerring wisdom and ineffable love! Here we are often baffled at the Lord's dispensations; we cannot fathom His ways:—like the well of Sychar, they are deep, and we have nothing to draw with. But soon the "mystery of God will be finished;" the enigmatical "seals," with all their inner meanings, opened. When that "morning without clouds" shall break, each soul will be like the angel standing in the sun—there will be no shadow; all will be perfect day!

Believer, be still! The dealings of thy Heavenly Father may seem dark to thee; there may seem now to be no golden fringe, no "bright light in the clouds;" but a day of disclosures is at hand. "Take it on trust a little while." An earthly child takes *on trust* what his father tells him: when he reaches maturity, much that was baffling to his infant comprehension is explained. Thou art in this world in the nonage of thy being—Eternity is the soul's immortal manhood. *There*, every dealing will be vindicated. It will lose all its "darkness" when bathed in the floods "of the excellent glory!"

Ah! instead of thus being as weaned children, how apt are we to exercise ourselves in matters too high for us? not content with knowing that our Father *wills* it, but presumptuously seeking to know *how* it is, and *why* it is. If it be unfair to pronounce on the unfinished and incompleted works of man; if the painter, or sculptor, or artificer, would shrink from having his labours judged of when in a rough, unpolished, immatured state; how much more so with the works of God? How we should honour Him by a simple, confiding, unreserved submission to His will,—contented patiently to wait the fulfilment of this "*hereafter*" promise, when all the lights and shadows in the now half-finished picture will be blended and melted into one harmonious whole,—when all the now disjointed stones in the temple will be seen to fit into their appointed place, giving unity, and compactness, and symmetry, to all the building.

And who is it that speaks these living "words," "What *I* do?" It is He who died for us? who now lives for us! Blessed Jesus! Thou mayest *do* much that our blind hearts would like *undone*,—"terrible things in righteousness which we looked not for." The heaviest (what we may be tempted to call the severest) cross Thou canst lay upon us we shall regard as only the *apparent* severity of unutterable and unalterable love. Eternity will unfold how *all*, *all* was needed; that nothing else, nothing less, could have done! If not now, at least then, the deliberate verdict on a calm retrospect of life will be this,—

"THE WORD OF THE LORD IS RIGHT, AND ALL HIS WORKS ARE DONE IN TRUTH."

5TH DAY.

"Remember the words of the Lord Jesus, how He said"—

"Herein is my Father glorified, that *ye bear much fruit.*"
—John xv. 8.

The Father Glorified.

WHEN surveying the boundless ocean of covenant mercy—every wave chiming, "God is Love!"—does the thought ever present itself, "What can I do for this great Being who hath done so much for me? Recompence I cannot! No more can my purest services add one iota to His underived glory, than the tiny taper can add to the blaze of the sun at noonday, or a drop of water to the boundless ocean. Yet, wondrous thought! from this worthless soul of mine there may roll in a revenue of glory which He who loves the broken and contrite spirit will "not despise." "*Herein is my Father glorified, that ye bear much fruit.*"

Reader! are you a fruit-bearer in your Lord's vineyard? Are you seeking to make life one grand act of consecration to His glory—one thank-offering for His unmerited love. You may be unable to exhibit much fruit in the eye of the world. Your circumstances and position in life may forbid you to point to any splendid services, or laborious and imposing efforts in the cause of God. It matters not. It is often those fruits that are unseen and unknown to man, ripening in seclusion, that He values most;—the quiet, lowly walk—patience and submission—gentleness and humility—putting yourself unreservedly in His hands—willing to be led by Him even in darkness—saying, Not *my* will, but *Thy* will:—the unselfish spirit, the meek bearing of an injury, the unostentatious kindness,—these are some of the "fruits" which your Heavenly Father loves, and by which He is glorified.

Perchance it may be with you the season of trial, the chamber of protracted sickness, the time of desolating bereavement, some furnace seven times heated. Herein, too, you may sweetly glorify your God. Never is your Heavenly Father *more* glorified by His children on earth, than when, in the midst of these furnace-fires, He listens to nothing but the gentle breathings of confiding faith and love,—"Let Him do what seemeth good unto Him." Yes, you can there glorify Him in a way which angels cannot do in a world where no trial is. They can glorify God only with the *crown;* you can glorify Him with the *cross* and the prospect of the *crown* together! Ah, if He be dealing severely with you—if He, as the great Husbandman, be pruning His vines, lopping their boughs, stripping off their luxuriant branches and "beautiful rods!" remember the end! —"He purgeth it, that it may bring forth *more* fruit," and "*Herein* is my Father glorified!

Be it yours to lie passive in His hands, saying in unmurmuring resignation, Father, glorify Thy name! Glorify Thyself, whether by giving or taking, filling my cup or "emptying me from vessel to vessel!" Let me know no will but Thine. Angels possess no higher honour and privilege than glorifying the God before whom they cast their crowns. How blessed to be able thus to claim brotherhood with the spirits in the upper sanctuary! nay, more, to be associated with the Saviour Himself in the theme of His own exalted joy, when he said, "*I* have *glorified* Thee on earth!"

"THESE THINGS HAVE I SPOKEN UNTO YOU, THAT MY JOY MIGHT REMAIN IN YOU, AND THAT YOUR JOY MIGHT BE FULL."

6TH DAY.

"Remember the words of the Lord Jesus, how He said"—

"The very hairs of your head are all numbered."—Matt. x. 30.

The Tender Solicitude.

WHAT a "word" is this! All that befals you, to the very numbering of your hairs, is known to God! Nothing can happen by accident or chance. Nothing can elude His inspection. The fall of the forest leaf—the fluttering of the insect—the waving of the angel's wing—the annihilation of a world,—all are equally noted by Him. Man speaks of great things and small things—God knows no such distinction.

How especially comforting to think of this tender solicitude with reference to his own covenant people—that He metes out their joys and their sorrows! Every sweet, every bitter is ordained by Him. Even "*wearisome* nights" are "*appointed*." Not a pang I feel, not a tear I shed but is known to Him. What are called "dark dealings" are the ordinations of undeviating faithfulness. Man *may* err—his ways are often crooked; "but as for God, *His* way is perfect!" He puts my tears into His bottle. Every moment the everlasting arms are underneath and around me. He keeps me "as the apple of His eye." He "bears" me "as a man beareth his own son!"

Do I look to the future? Is there much of uncertainty and mystery hanging over it? It may be, much premonitory of evil. Trust Him. All is marked out for me. Dangers will be averted; bewildering mazes will show themselves to be interlaced and interweaved with mercy. "He keepeth the feet of His saints." A hair of their head will not be touched. He leads sometimes darkly, sometimes sorrowfully; most frequently by cross and circuitous ways we ourselves would not have chosen; but *always* wisely, *always* tenderly. With all its mazy windings and turnings, its roughness and ruggedness, the believer's is not only *a* right way, but THE right way—the best which covenant love and wisdom could select. "Nothing," says Jeremy Taylor, "does so establish the mind amidst the rollings and turbulence of present things, as both a look above them and a look beyond them; above them, to the steady and good hand by which they are ruled; and beyond them, to the sweet and beautiful end to which, by that hand, they will be brought." "The Great Counsellor," says Thomas Brooks, "puts clouds and darkness round about Him, bidding us follow at His beck through the cloud, promising an eternal and uninterrupted sunshine on the other side." On that "other side" we shall see how every apparent rough blast has been hastening our barks nearer the desired haven.

Well may I commit the keeping of my soul to Jesus in well-doing, as unto a faithful Creator. He gave *Himself* for me. This transcendent pledge of love is the guarantee for the bestowment of every other needed blessing. Oh, blessed thought! my sorrows numbered by the Man of Sorrows; my tears counted by Him who shed first His tears and then His blood for *me*. He will impose no needless burden, and exact no unnecessary sacrifice. There was no redundant drop in the cup of His own sufferings; neither will there be in that of His people. "Though He slay me, yet will I trust in Him."

"WHEREFORE COMFORT ONE ANOTHER WITH THESE WORDS."

7TH DAY.

"Remember the words of the Lord Jesus, how He said"—

"I am the good shepherd, and know my sheep, and am known of mine."—John x. 14.

The Good Shepherd.

"THE Good Shepherd" —well can the sheep who know His voice attest the truthfulness and faithfulness of this endearing name and word. Where would they have been through eternity, had He not left His throne of light and glory, travelling down to this dark valley of the curse, and giving His life a ransom for many? Think of His love to each separate member of the flock—wandering over pathless wilds with unwearied patience and unquenchable ardour, ceasing not the pursuit *until* He finds it. Think of His love *now*—"I AM the Good Shepherd." Still that tender eye of watchfulness following the guilty wanderers—the glories of heaven and the songs of angels unable to dim or alter His affection;—the music of the words, at this moment coming as sweetly from His lips as when first He uttered them—"I know my sheep." Every individual believer—the weakest, the weariest, the faintest—claims His attention. His loving eye follows me day by day out to the wilderness—marks out my pasture, studies my wants, and trials, and sorrows, and perplexities—every steep ascent, every brook, every winding path, every thorny thicket. "He goeth before them." It is not rough driving, but gentle guiding. He does not take them over an unknown road; He himself has trodden it before. He hath drunk of every "brook by the way;" He himself hath "suffered being tempted;" He is "able to succour them that are tempted." He seems to say, "Fear not; I cannot lead you wrong; follow me in the bleak waste, the blackened wilderness, as well as by the green pastures and the still waters. Do you ask why I have left the sunny side of the valley—carpeted with flowers, and bathed in sunshine—leading you to some high mountain apart, some cheerless spot of sorrow? Trust me, I will lead you by paths you have not known, but they are all known *to* me, and selected *by* me—'Follow thou me.'"

"And am known of mine!" Reader! canst thou subscribe to these closing words of this gracious utterance? Dost thou "know" *Him* in all the glories of His person, in all the completeness of His finished work, in all the tenderness and unutterable love of His every dealing towards thee?

It has been remarked by Palestine travellers, that not only do the sheep there follow the guiding shepherd, but even while cropping the herbage as they go along, they look wistfully up to see that they are near him. Is this thine attitude—"*looking unto Jesus?*" "In all thy ways acknowledge Him, and he will direct thy paths." Leave the future to His providing. "The Lord is my Shepherd; I shall not want." *I shall not want!*—it has been beautifully called "the bleating of Messiah's sheep." Take it as thy watchword during thy wilderness wanderings, till grace be perfected in glory. Let this be the record of thy simple faith and unwavering trust, "These are they who *follow*, whithersoever He sees meet to guide them."

"THE SHEEP FOLLOW HIM, FOR THEY KNOW HIS VOICE."

8TH DAY.

"Remember the words of the Lord Jesus, how He said"—

"And I will pray the Father, and He shall give you another Comforter, that he may abide with you for ever."—John xiv. 16.

The Abiding Comforter.

WHEN one beloved earthly friend is taken away, how the heart is drawn out towards those that remain! Jesus was now about to leave His sorrowing disciples. He directs them to one whose presence would fill up the vast blank His own absence was to make. His name was, *The Comforter;* His mission was, "to abide with them for ever." Accordingly, no sooner had the gates of heaven closed on their ascended Lord, than, in fulfilment of His own gracious promise, the bereaved and orphaned Church was baptized with Pentecostal fire. "When I depart, I will send Him unto you."

Reader, do you realize your privilege —living under the dispensation of the Spirit? Is it your daily prayer that He may come down in all the plenitude of His heavenly graces on your soul, even "as rain upon the mown grass, and showers that water the earth?" You cannot live without Him; there can be not one heavenly aspiration, not one breathing of love, not one upward glance of faith, without His gracious influences. Apart from him, there is no preciousness in the Word, no blessing in ordinances, no permanent sanctifying results in affliction. As the angel directed Hagar to the hidden spring, this blessed agent, true to His name and office, directs His people to the waters of comfort, giving new glory to the promises, investing the Saviour's character and work with new loveliness and beauty.

How precious is the title which this "Word of Jesus" gives Him—THE

COMFORTER! What a word for a sorrowing world! The Church militant has its tent pitched in a "valley of *tears*." The name of the divine visitant who comes to her and ministers to her wants, is *Comforter*. Wide is the family of the afflicted, but He has a healing balm for all—the weak, the tempted, the sick, the sorrowing, the bereaved, the dying! How different from other "sons of consolation?" *Human friends*—a look may alienate; adversity may estrange; death must separate! The "Word of Jesus" speaks of One whose attribute and prerogative is to "abide with us for ever;" superior to all vicissitudes—surviving death itself!

And surely if anything else can endear His mission of love to His Church, it is that He comes direct from God, as the fruit and gift of *Jesus' intercession*—"*I* will pray the Father." This holy dove of peace and comfort is let out by the hand of Jesus from the ark of covenant mercy within the veil! Nor is the gift more glorious than it is free. Does the word, the look, of a suffering child get the eye and the heart of an *earthly* father? "If ye then, being evil, know how to give good gifts unto your children, how much more shall your Father in heaven give the Holy Spirit unto them that ask Him?" It is He who makes these "words of Jesus" "winged words."

"HE SHALL BRING ALL THINGS TO YOUR REMEMBRANCE, WHATSOEVER I HAVE SAID UNTO YOU."

9TH DAY.

"Remember the words of the Lord Jesus, how He said"—

"Neither do I condemn thee; go and sin no more."—John viii. 11.

The Gracious Verdict. How much more tender is Jesus than the tenderest of earthly friends? The Apostles, in a moment of irritation would have called down fire from heaven on obstinate sinners. Their Master rebuked the unkind suggestion. Peter, the trusted but treacherous disciple, expected nothing but harsh and merited reproof for faithlessness. He who knew well how that heart would be bowed with penitential sorrow, sends first the kindest of messages, and then the gentlest of rebukes, "Lovest thou me?" The watchmen in the Canticles smote the bride, tore off her veil, and loaded her with reproaches. When she found her lost Lord, there was not one word of upbraiding! "So slow is He to anger," says an illustrious believer, "so ready to forgive, that when His prophets lost all patience with the people so as to make intercession *against* them, yet even then could He not be got to cast off this people whom He foreknew, for his great name's sake."

The guilty sinner to whom He speaks this comforting "word," was frowned upon by her accusers. But, if others spurned her from their presence, "*Neither do I condemn thee.*" Well it is to fall into the hands of this blessed Saviour-God, for great are His mercies.

Are we to infer from this, that He winks at sin? Far from it. His blood, His work—Bethlehem, and Calvary, refute the thought! Ere the guilt even of one solitary soul could be washed out, He had to descend from His everlasting throne to agonise on the accursed tree. But this "word of Jesus" is a word of tender encouragement to every sincere, broken-hearted penitent, that crimson sins, and scarlet sins, are no barriers to a free, full, everlasting forgiveness. The Israelite of old, gasping in his agony in the sands of the wilderness, had but to "*look* and *live;*" and still does He say, "Look unto me, and be ye saved, all the ends of the earth." Upreared by the side of his own cross there was a monumental column for all Time, only second to itself in wonder. Over the head of the dying felon is the superscription written for despairing guilt and trembling penitence, "This is a faithful saying, and worthy of all acceptation, that Jesus Christ came into the world to save sinners." "He never yet," says Charnock, "put out a dim candle that was lighted at the Sun of Righteousness." "Whatever our guiltiness be," says Rutherford, "yet when it falleth into the sea of God's mercy, it is but like a drop of blood fallen into the great ocean."

Reader, you may be the chief of sinners, or it may be the chief of backsliders; your soul may have started aside like a broken bow. As the bankrupt is afraid to look into his books, you may be afraid to look into your own heart. You are hovering on the verge of despair. Conscience, and the memory of unnumbered sins, is uttering the desponding verdict, "I condemn thee." Jesus has a kinder word—a more cheering declaration—"*I* condemn thee *not:* go, and sin no more!"

"AND ALL WONDERED AT THE GRACIOUS WORDS THAT PROCEEDED OUT OF HIS MOUTH."

10TH DAY.

"Remember the words of the Lord Jesus, how He said"—

"Whosoever shall do the will of my Father which is in heaven, the same is my brother, and my sister, and mother."—Matt. xii. 50.

The Wondrous Relationship. As if no solitary earthly type were enough to image forth the love of Jesus, He assembles into one verse a group of the tenderest earthly relationships. Human affection has to focus its loveliest hues, but all is too little to afford an exponent of the depth and intensity of *His*. "As one whom his *mother* comforteth;" "my *sister*, my *spouse*." He is "*Son*," "*Brother*" "*Friend*"—all in one; "cleaving closer than any brother."

And can we wonder at such language? Is it merely figurative, expressive of more than the reality?—He gave *Himself* for us; after that pledge of His affection we must cease to marvel at any expression of the interest He feels in us. Anything He can *say* or *do* is infinitely less than what He *has done.*

Believer! art thou solitary and desolate? Has bereavement severed earthly ties? Has the grave made forced estrangements,—sundered the closest links of earthly affection? In Jesus thou hast filial and fraternal love combined; He is the Friend of friends, whose presence and fellowship compensates for all losses, and supplies all blanks; "He setteth the solitary in families." If thou art orphaned, friendless, comfortless here, remember there is in the Elder Brother on the Throne a love deep as the unfathomed ocean, boundless as Eternity?

And who are those who can claim the blessedness spoken of under this wondrous imagery? On whom does He lavish this unutterable affection? No outward profession will purchase it. No church, no priest, no ordinances, no denominational distinctions. It is on those who are possessed of *holy characters.* "He that doeth the will of my Father which is in heaven!" He who reflects the mind of Jesus; imbibes His Spirit; takes His Word as the regulator of his daily walk, and makes His glory the great end of his being; he who lives *to* God and *with* God, and *for* God; the humble, lowly, Christ-like, Heaven-seeking Christian;—he it is who can claim as his own this wondrous heritage of love! If it be a worthy object of ambition to be loved by the good and the great on earth, what must it be to have an eye of love ever beaming upon us from the Throne, in comparison of which the attachment here of brother, sister, kinsman, friend—all combined—pales like the stars before the rising sun! Though we are often ashamed to call Him "Brother," "He is not ashamed to call us *brethren.*" He looks down on pocr worms, and says,

"*The same* is my mother, and sister, and brother!" "I will write upon them," He says in another place, "my new name." Just as we write our name on a book to tell that it belongs to us; so Jesus would write His own name on *us*, the wondrous volumes of His grace, that they may be read and pondered by principalities and powers.

Have we "known and believed this love of God?" Ah, how poor has been the requital! Who cannot subscribe to the words of one, whose name was in all the churches,—"Thy love has been as a shower; the return but a dew-drop, and that dew-drop stained with sin."

"IF A MAN LOVE ME, HE WILL KEEP MY WORDS; AND MY FATHER WILL LOVE HIM, AND WE WILL COME UNTO HIM, AND MAKE OUR ABODE WITH HIM."

11TH DAY.

"Remember the words of the Lord Jesus, how He said"—

"I will not leave you comfortless: I will come to you."— John xiv. 18.

The Befriended Orphans.

DOES the Christian's path lie all the way through Beulah? Nay, he is forewarned it is to be one of "much tribulation." He has his Marahs as well as his Elims—his valleys of Baca as well as his grapes of Eschol. Often is he left unbefriended to bear the brunt of the storm—his gourds fading when most needed—his sun going down while it is yet day—his happy home and happy heart darkened in a moment with sorrows with which a stranger (with which often a *brother*) cannot intermeddle. There is *One* Brother "born for adversity," who *can*. How often has that voice broken with its silvery accents the muffled stillness of the sick-chamber or death-chamber! "'*I* will not leave you comfortless:' the world *may*, friends *may*, the desolations of bereavement and death *may;* but *I will not;* you will be alone, yet *not* alone, for I your Saviour and your God will be with you!"

Jesus seems to have an especial love and affection for His orphaned and comfortless people. A father loves his sick and sorrowing child most; of all his household, he occupies most of his thoughts. Christ seems to delight to lavish His deepest sympathy on "him that hath ho helper." It is in the hour of sorrow His people have found Him most precious; it is in "the wilderness" He speaks most "comfortably unto them;" He gives them "their vineyards from thence:" in the places they least expected, wells of heavenly consolation break forth at their feet. As Jonathan of old, when faint and weary, had his strength revived by the honey he found dropping in the tangled thicket: so the faint and woe-worn children of God find "honey in the wood"—everlasting consolation dropping from the tree of life, in the midst of the thorniest thickets of affliction.

Comfortless ones, be comforted! Jesus often makes you *portionless* here, to drive you to Himself, the *everlasting portion*. He often dries every rill and fountain of earthly bliss, that He may lead you to say, "All my springs are in Thee." "He seems intent," says one who could speak from experience, "to fill up every gap love has been forced to make; one of his errands from heaven was to bind up the broken-hearted." How beautifully in one amazing verse does he conjoin the depth and tenderness of his comfort with the certainty of it—"As one whom his mother comforteth, so will I comfort you, and ye SHALL be comforted!"

Ah, how many would not have their

wilderness-state altered, with all its trials, and gloom, and sorrow, just that they might enjoy the unutterable sympathy and love of this Comforter of the comfortless, one ray of whose approving smile can dispel the deepest earthly gloom? As the clustering constellations shine with intensest lustre in the midnight sky, so these "words of Jesus" come out like ministering angels in the deep dark night of earthly sorrow. We may see no beauty in them when the world is sunny and bright; but He has laid them up in store for us for the dark and cloudy day."

"THESE THINGS HAVE I TOLD YOU, THAT WHEN THE TIME COMETH, YE MAY REMEMBER THAT I TOLD YOU OF THEM."

12TH DAY.

"Remember the words of the Lord Jesus, how He said"—

"In the world ye shall have tribulation: but be of good cheer; I have overcome the world."—John xvi. 33.

The World Conquered.

AND shall I be afraid of a world already conquered? The Almighty Victor, within view of His Crown, turns round to His faint and weary soldiers, and bids them take courage. They are not fighting their way through untried enemies. The God-Man Mediator "*knows* their sorrows." "He was in *all points* tempted." "Both He (*i. e.*, Christ) who sanctifieth, and they (His people) who are sanctified, are all of one (nature)." As the great Precursor, he heads the pilgrim band, saying "I will show you the path of life." The way to heaven is consecrated by His footprints. Every thorn that wounds *them*, has wounded *Him* before. Every cross they can bear, he has borne before. Every tear they shed, He has shed before. There is one respect, indeed, in which the identity fails,—He was "yet without sin;" but this recoil of His Holy nature from moral evil gives Him a deeper and intenser sensibility towards those who have still corruption within responding to temptation without.

Reader! are you ready to faint under your tribulations? Is it a seducing world—a wandering, wayward heart? "Consider *Him* that endured!" Listen to your adorable Redeemer, stooping from His Throne, and saying, "*I* have overcome the world." He came forth unscathed from its snares. With the same heavenly weapon He bids you wield, three times did he repel the Tempter, saying, "It is written."—Is it some crushing trial, or overwhelming grief? He is "*acquainted* with *grief*." He, the mighty Vine, knows the minutest fibres of sorrow in the branches; when the pruning knife touches *them*, it touches *Him*. "He has gone," says a tried sufferer, "through every class in our wilderness school." He loves to bring His people into untried and perplexing places, that they may seek out the guiding pillar, and prize its radiance. He puts them on the darkening waves, that they may follow the guiding light hung out astern from the only Bark of pure and unsullied Humanity that was ever proof against the storm.

Be assured there is disguised love in all He does. He who knows us infinitely better than we know ourselves, often puts a thorn in our nest to drive us to the wing, that we may not be grovellers forever. "It is," says Evans, "upon the smooth ice we slip," the rough path is safest for the feet." The tearless and undimmed eye is not to be coveted *here; that* is reserved for heaven!

Who can tell what muffled and disguised "needs be" there may lurk under these world-tribulations? His true spiritual seed are often planted deep in the soil; they have to make their way through a load of sorrow before they reach the surface; but their roots are thereby the firmer and deeper struck. Had it not been for these lowly and needed "depths," they might have rushed up as feeble saplings, and succumbed to the first blast. He often leads His people still, as he led them of old, to "a high mountain apart;" but it is to a *high* mountain—*above the world;* and, better still, He who Himself hath overcome the world, leadeth them there, and speaketh comfortably unto them.

"I HOPE IN THY WORD."

13TH DAY.

"Remember the words of the Lord Jesus, how He said"—

"Fear not, little flock; it is your Father's good pleasure to give you the kingdom."—Luke xii. 32.

The Little Flock.

THE music of the Shepherd's voice again! Another comforting "word," and how tender! *his* flock a *little* flock, a *feeble* flock, a *fearful* flock, but a *beloved* flock, loved of the Father, enjoying His "good pleasure," and soon to be a *glorified* flock, safe in the fold, secure within the kingdom! How does He quiet their fears and misgivings? As they stand panting on the bleak mountain side, He points His crook upwards to the bright and shining gates of glory, and says, "It is your Father's good pleasure to give you these!" What gentle words! What a blessed consummation! Gracious Saviour, Thy *gentleness* hath made me *great!*

That kingdom is the believer's by irreversible and inalienable charter-right—"I appoint unto you" (by covenant), says Jesus in another place, "a kingdom, as my Father hath appointed unto me." It is as sure as everlasting love and almighty power can make it. Satan, the great foe of the kingdom, may be injecting foul misgivings, and doubts, and fears as to your security; but he cannot denude you of your purchased immunities. He must first pluck the crown from the Brow upon the Throne, before he can weaken or impair this sure word of promise. If "it pleased the Lord" to *bruise* the Shepherd, it will surely please Him to make happy the purchased flock. If He "smote" His "Fellow" when the sheep were scattered, surely it will rejoice Him, for the Shepherd's sake, "to turn His hand upon the little ones."

Believers, think of this! "It is your Father's good pleasure." The Good

Shepherd, in leading you across the intervening mountains, shows you signals and memorials of paternal grace studding all the way. He may "lead you about" in your way thither. He led the children of Israel of old out of Egypt to their promised kingdom,—how? By forty years' wilderness-discipline and privations. But trust Him; dishonour Him not with guilty doubts and fears. Look not back on your dark, stumbling paths, nor within on your fitful and vacillating heart; but forwards to the land that is far off. How earnestly God desires your salvation! What a heaping together of similar tender "words" with that which is here addressed to us? The Gospel seems like a palace full of opened windows, from each of which He issues an invitation, declaring that He has no pleasure in our death—but rather that we would turn and live!

Let the melody of the Shepherd's

reed fall gently on your ear,—"It is your Father's good pleasure." I have given you, He seems to say, the best proof that it is *mine*. In order to purchase that kingdom, I died for you! But it is also *His:* "As a shepherd seeketh out his flock in the day that he is among his sheep that are scattered, so," says God, "will I seek out my sheep, and will deliver them out of all places where they have been scattered in the cloudy and dark day." Fear not, then, little flock! though yours for a while should be the bleak mountain and sterile waste, seeking your way Zionward, it may be "with torn fleeces and bleeding feet;" for,

"IT IS NOT THE WILL OF YOUR FATHER WHICH IS IN HEAVEN, THAT ONE OF THESE LITTLE ONES SHOULD PERISH."

14TH DAY.

"Remember the words of the Lord Jesus, how He said"—

"If any man thirst, let him come unto me, and drink."— John vii. 37.

The Unlimited Offer.

ONE of the most gracious "words" that ever "proceeded out of the mouth of God!" The time it was uttered was an impressive one; it was on "the last, the great day" of the Feast of Tabernacles, when a denser multitude than on any of the seven preceding ones were assembled together. The golden bowl, according to custom, had probably just been filled with the waters of Siloam, and was being carried up to the Temple amid the acclamations of the crowd, when the Saviour of the world seized the opportunity of speaking to them some truths of momentous import. Many, doubtless, were the "words of Jesus" uttered on the previous days, but the most important is reserved for the last. What, then, is the great closing theme on which He rivets the attention of this vast auditory, and which He would have them carry away to their distant homes? It is, *The freeness of His own great salvation*—"If any man thirst, let him come unto me and drink."

Reader, do you discredit the reality of this gracious offer? Are your legion sins standing as a barrier between you and a Saviour's proffered mercy? Do you feel as if you cannot come "just as you are;" that some partial cleansing, some preparatory reformation must take place before you can venture to the living fountain? Nay, "*if any man.*" What is freer than water?—The poorest beggar may drink "without money" the wayside pool. *That* is your Lord's own picture of His own glorious salvation; you are invited to come, "without one plea," in all your poverty and want, your weakness and unworthiness. Remember the Redeemer's saying to the woman of Samaria. She was the chief of sinners—profligate—hardened—degraded; but He made no condition, no qualification; *simple believing* was all that was required,—"If thou knewest the gift of God," thou wouldst have asked, and He would have given thee "living water."

But is there not, after all, *one* condition mentioned in this "word of Jesus?"—"*If* any man *thirst.*" You may have the depressing consciousness that you experience no such ardent longings after holiness,—no feeling of your affecting need of the Saviour. But is not this very conviction of your want an indication of a feeble longing after Christ? If you are saying, "I have nothing to draw with, and the well is deep," He who makes offer of the salvation-stream will Himself fill your empty vessel,—"He satisfieth the *longing* soul with goodness."

"Jesus *stood* and *cried*." It is the solitary instance recorded of Him of whom it is said, "He shall *not* strive nor cry," lifting up "His voice in the streets." But it was truth of surpassing interest and magnitude He had to proclaim. It was a declaration, moreover, specially dear to him. As it formed the theme of this ever-memorable *sermon* during His public ministry, so when He was sealing up the inspired record—the last utterances of His voice on earth, till that voice shall be heard again on the throne, contained the same life-giving invitation,—"Let him that is athirst come, and whosoever will, let him take of the water of life freely." Oh! as the echoes of that gracious saying—this blast of the silver trumpet—are still sounding to the ends of the world, may this be the recorded result,

"AS HE SPAKE THESE WORDS, MANY BELIEVED ON HIM."

15TH DAY.

"Remember the words of the Lord Jesus, how He said"—

"My yoke is easy, and my burden is light."—Matt. xi. 30.

The Joyful Servitude.

CAN the same be said of Satan, or sin? With regard to *them*, how faithfully true rather is the converse—"my yoke is *heavy*, and my burden is *griev ous!*" Christ's service is a happy service, the *only* happy one; and even when there is a cross to carry, or a yoke to bear, it is His own appointment. "*My* yoke." It is sent by no untried friend. Nay, He who puts it on His people, bore this very yoke Himself. "He *carried* our sorrows." How blessed this feeling of holy servitude to so kind a Master! not like "dumb, driven cattle," goaded on, but *led*, and led often most tenderly when the yoke and the burden are upon us. The great apostle rarely speaks of himself under any other title but *one.* That *one* he seems to make his boast. He had much whereof he might glory;—he had been the instrument in saving thousands —he had spoken before kings—he had been in Cæsar's palace and Cæsar's presence—he had been caught up into the third heaven,—but in all his letters this is his joyful prefix and superscription, "The *Servant* (literally, *the slave*) of Jesus Christ!"

Reader! dost thou know this blessed servitude? Canst thou say with a joyful heart, "O Lord, truly I am Thy servant?" He is no hard taskmaster. Would Satan try to teach thee so? Let this be the refutation, "He loved me, and gave *Himself* for *me.*" True, the yoke is the appointed discipline he employs in training his children for immortality. But be comforted! "It is His tender hand that *puts* it on, and *keeps* it on." He will suit the yoke to the neck, and the neck to the yoke.

He will suit His grace to your trials. Nay, He will bring you even to be in love with these, when they bring along with them such gracious unfoldings of His own faithfulness and mercy. How His people need thus to be in heaviness through manifold temptations, to keep them meek and submissive! "Jeshurun (like a bullock unaccustomed to the harness, fed and pampered in the stall) waxed fat, and kicked." Never is there more gracious love than when God takes His own means to curb and subjugate, to humble us, and to prove us—bringing us out from ourselves, our likings, our confidences, our prosperity, and putting us under the needed YOKE.

And who has ever repented of that joyful servitude? Among all the ten thousand regrets that mingle with a dying hour, and oft bedew with bitter tears a dying pillow, who ever told of regrets and repentance here?

Tried believer, has He ever failed thee? Has His yoke been too grievous? Have thy tears been unalleviated—thy sorrows unsolaced—thy temptations above that thou wert able to bear? Ah! rather canst thou not testify, "The word of the Lord is tried;" I cast my burden upon Him, and He "sustained me?" How have seeming difficulties melted away! How has the yoke lost its heaviness, and the cross its bitterness, in the thought of whom thou wert bearing it for! There is a promised rest in the very carrying of the yoke; and a better rest remains for the weary and toil-worn when the appointed work is finished; for thus saith "that same Jesus,"

"TAKE MY YOKE UPON YOU, AND LEARN OF ME, . . .
AND YE SHALL FIND REST UNTO YOUR SOULS."

16TH DAY.

"Remember the words of the Lord Jesus, how He said"—

"As the Father hath loved me, so have I loved you."—John xv. 9.

The Measure of Love.

THIS is the most wondrous verse in the Bible. Who can sound the unimagined depths of that love which dwelt in the bosom of the Father from all eternity towards His Son?—and yet here is the Saviour's own exponent of His love towards His people!

There is no subject more profoundly mysterious than those mystic intercommunings between the first and second persons in the adorable Trinity before the world was. Scripture gives us only some dim and shadowy revelations regarding them—distant gleams of light, and no more. Let one suffice. "*Then* I was by Him, as one brought up with Him, and I was daily His delight, rejoicing always before Him."

We know that earthly affection is deepened and intensified by increased familiarity with its object. The friendship of yesterday is not the sacred, hallowed thing, which years of growing intercourse have matured. If we may with reverence apply this test to the highest type of holy affection, what must have been that interchange of love which the measureless lapse of Eternity had fostered—a love, moreover, not fitful, transient, vacillating, subject to altered tones and estranged looks—but pure, constant, untainted, without one shadow of turning! And yet, listen to the "words of Jesus," *As* the Father hath loved *me*, *so* have I loved *you!* It would have been infinitely more than we had reason to expect, if He had said, "As my Father hath loved ANGELS, so have I loved you." But the love borne to no finite beings is an appropriate symbol. Long before the birth of time or of worlds, that love existed. It was coeval with Eternity itself. Hear how the two themes of the Saviour's eternal rejoicing—the *love of His Father*, and His *love for sinners*—are grouped together; —"Rejoicing always before HIM, *and* in the habitable part of His *earth!*"

To complete the picture, we must take in a counterpart description of the *Father's* love to us;—"*Therefore* doth my Father love me," says Jesus in another place, "*because* I lay down my life!" God had an all-sufficiency in His love—He needed not the taper-love of creatures to add to His glory or happiness; but He seems to say, that so intense is His love for us, that He loves even His beloved Son *more* (if infinite love be capable of increase), because He laid down His life for the guilty! It is regarding the Redeemed it is said, "He shall *rest* in His love—He shall rejoice over *them* with singing."

In the assertion, "God is love," we

are left truly with no mere unproved averment regarding the existence of some abstract quality in the divine nature. "Herein," says an apostle, "perceive we THE LOVE,"—(it is added in our authorised version, "of God," but, as it has been remarked, "Our translators need not have added *whose* love, for there is but one such specimen") —"*because* He laid down His life for us." No expression of love can be wondered at after *this*. Ah, how miserable are our best affections compared with His! "*Our* love is but the reflection—cold as the moon; *His* is as the Sun." Shall we refuse to love Him more in return, who hath *first* loved, and so *loved us?*

"NEVER MAN SPAKE LIKE THIS MAN."

17TH DAY.

"Remember the words of the Lord Jesus, how He said"—

"Only believe."—Mark v. 36.

The Brief Gospel.

THE briefest of the "words of Jesus," but one of the most comforting. They contain the essence and epitome of all saving truth.

Reader, is *Satan* assailing thee with tormenting fears? Is the thought of thy sins—the guilty past—coming up in terrible memorial before thee, almost tempting thee to give way to hopeless despondency? Fear not! A gentle voice whispers in thine ear,—"*Only believe.*" "Thy sins are great, but my grace and merits are greater. 'Only believe' that I died for thee—that I am living for thee and pleading for thee, and that 'the faithful saying' is as 'faithful' as ever, and as 'worthy of all acceptation' as ever."—Art thou a *backslider?* Didst thou once run well? Has thine own guilty apostacy alienated and estranged thee from that face which was once all love, and that service which was once all delight? Art thou breathing in broken-hearted sorrow over the holy memories of a close walk with God—"Oh that it were with me as in months past, when the candle of the Lord did shine?" "*Only believe.*" Take this thy mournful soliloquy, and convert it into a prayer. "Only believe" the word of Him whose ways are not as man's ways—"Return, ye backsliding children, and I will heal your backsliding."—Art thou beaten down with some heavy *trial?* have thy fondest schemes been blown upon—thy fairest blossoms been withered in the bud? has wave after wave been rolling in upon thee? hath the Lord forgotten to be gracious? Hear the "word of Jesus" resounding amid the thickest midnight of gloom—penetrating even through the vaults of the dead—"Believe, *only believe.*" There is an infinite *reason* for the trial—a lurking thorn that required removal, a gracious lesson that required teaching. The dreadful severing blow was dealt in love. God will be glorified in it, and your own soul made the better for it. Patiently wait till the light of immortality be reflected on a receding world. Here you must take His dealings on trust. The word of Jesus to you now is, "*Only believe.*" The word of Jesus in eternity (every inner meaning and undeveloped purpose being unfolded), "Said I not unto thee that if thou wouldest *but* BELIEVE, thou shouldst SEE the glory of God?"—Are you fearful and agitated in *the prospect of death?* Through fear of the last enemy, have you been all your lifetime subject to bondage?—"*Only believe.*" "As thy day is, so shall thy strength be." Dying grace will be given when a dying hour comes. In the dark river a sustaining arm will be underneath you, deeper than the deepest and darkest wave. Ere you know it, the darkness will be past, the true Light shining,—the whisper of faith in the nether valley," "Believe! believe!" exchanged for angel-voices exclaiming, as you enter the portals of glory, "No longer through a glass darkly, but now face to face!"

Yes! "Jesus Himself had no higher remedy for sin, for sorrow, and for suffering, than those two words convey. At the utmost extremity of His own distress, and of His disciples' wretchedness, He could only say, 'Let not your heart be troubled: ye believe in God, believe also in me.' 'Believe, only believe.'"

"LORD, I BELIEVE, HELP THOU MINE UNBELIEF."

18TH DAY.

"Remember the words of the Lord Jesus, how He said"—

"Be of good cheer: it is I; be not afraid."—Mark vi. 50.

The Great Calm. "It is I," (or as our old version has it, more in accordance with the original), "I AM! be not afraid!" Jesus lives! His people may dispel their misgivings —Omnipotence treads the waves! To sense it may seem at times to be otherwise; wayward accident and chance may appear to regulate human allotments; but not so: "The Lord's voice is upon the waters,"—He sits at the helm guiding the tempest-tossed bark, and guiding it well.

How often does He come to us as He did to the disciples in that midnight hour when all seems lost—"in the fourth watch of the night,"—when we least looked for Him; or when, like the shipwrecked apostle, "for days together neither sun nor stars appeared, and no small tempest lay on us; when all hope that we should be saved seemed to be taken away,"—how often *just at that moment*, is the "word of Jesus" heard floating over the billows!

Believer, art thou in trouble? listen to the voice in the storm, "Fear not, *I* AM." That voice, like Joseph's of old to his brethren, may *seem* rough, but there are gracious undertones of love. "It is I," he seems to say; It *was* I, that roused the storm; It is I, who when it has done its work, will calm it, and say, "Peace, be still." Every wave rolls at My bidding—every trial is My appointment—all have some gracious end; they are not sent to dash you against the sunken rocks, but to waft you nearer heaven. Is it *sickness?* I am He who bare your sickness; the weary wasted frame, and the nights of languishing, were sent by Me. Is it *bereavement?* I am "the Brother" born for adversity—the loved and lost were plucked away by Me. Is it *death?* I AM the "Abolisher of death," seated by your side to calm the waves of ebbing life; it is *I*, about to fetch My pilgrims *home*—It is My voice that speaks, "The Master is come, and calleth for thee."

Reader, thou wilt have reason yet to praise thy God for every one such storm! This is the history of every heavenly voyager: "*So* He bringeth them to their desired haven." "*So!*" That word, in all its unknown and diversified meaning, is in *His* hand. He suits His dealings to every case. "*So!*" With some it is through quiet seas unfretted by one buffeting wave. "*So!*" With others it is "mounting up to heaven, and going down again to the deep." But whatever be the leading and the discipline, here is the grand consummation, "*So* He bringeth them unto their desired haven." It might have been with thee the moanings of an eternal night-blast—no lull or pause in the storm; but soon the darkness will be past, and the hues of morn tipping the shores of glory!

And what, then, should your attitude be? "Looking unto Jesus" (literally, looking *from unto*); looking away from self, and sin, and human props and refuges and confidences, and fixing the eye of unwavering and unflinching faith on a reigning Saviour. Ah, how a real quickening sight of Christ dispels all guilty fears! The Roman keepers of old were affrighted, and became as dead men. The lowly Jewish women feared not; why? "*I know that ye seek Jesus!*" Reader, let thy weary spirit fold itself to rest under the composing "word" of a gracious Saviour, saying—

"I WAIT FOR THE LORD, MY SOUL DOTH WAIT, AND IN HIS WORD DO I HOPE."

19TH DAY.

"Remember the words of the Lord Jesus, how He said"—

"Peace I leave with you, my peace I give unto you: not as the world giveth, give I unto you."—John xiv. 27.

The Dying Legacy.

How we treasure the last sayings of a dying parent! How specially cherished and memorable are his last looks and last words! Here are the last words—the parting legacy—of a dying Saviour. It is a legacy of *peace*.

What peace is this? It is His own purchase—a peace arising out of free forgiveness through His precious blood. It is sung in concert with "Glory to God in the highest"—a peace made as sure to us as eternal power and infinite love *can make* it! It is *peace* the soul wants. Existence is one long-drawn sigh after repose. *That* is nowhere else to be found, but through the blood of His cross! "Being justified by faith, we *have* peace with God." "He giveth his beloved *rest!*"

How different from the false and counterfeit peace in which so many are content to live, and content to die! The world's peace is all well, so long as prosperity lasts—so long as the stream runs smooth, and the sky is clear; but when the cataract is at hand, or the storm is gathering, where is it? It is *gone!* There is no calculating on its permanency. Often when the cup is fullest, there is the trembling apprehension that in one brief moment it may be dashed to the ground. The soul may be saying to itself, "Peace, peace;" but, like the writing on the sand, it may be obliterated by the first wave of adversity. But, "Not as the world giveth!" The peace of the believer is deep—calm — lasting — *ever*lasting. The world, with all its blandishments, cannot give it. The world, with all its vicissitudes and fluctuations, cannot take it away!

It is brightest in the hour of trial; it lights up the final valley-gloom. "Mark the perfect man, and behold the upright, for the end of that man is peace." Yes! how often is the believer's deathbed like the deep calm repose of a summer-evening's sky, when all nature is hushed to rest; the departing soul, like the vanishing sun, peacefully disappearing only to shine in another and brighter hemisphere! "I seem," said Simeon on his deathbed, "to have nothing to do but to wait: there is now nothing but *peace*, the *sweetest peace*."

Believer! do you know this peace which passeth understanding? Is it "keeping (literally, '*garrisoning* as in a citadel') your heart?" Have you learnt the blessedness of waking up, morning after morning, and feeling, "I am at peace with my God;" of beholding by faith the true Aaron—the great High Priest—coming forth from "the holiest of all" to "bless His people with peace?" Waves of trouble may be murmuring around you, but they cannot touch you; you are in the rock-crevice athwart which the fiercest tornado sweeps by. Oh! leave not the making up of your peace with God to a dying hour! It will be a hard thing to smooth the death-pillow, if peace be left unsought till then. Make sure of it *now*. He, the true Melchisedec, is willing *now* to come forth to meet you with bread and wine—emblems of peaceful gospel blessings. All the "words of Jesus" are so many rills contributing to make your peace flow as a river;—"These things have I spoken unto you, that in Me ye might have peace."

"I WILL HEAR WHAT GOD THE LORD WILL SPEAK, FOR HE WILL SPEAK PEACE UNTO HIS PEOPLE AND TO HIS SAINTS."

20TH DAY.

"Remember the words of the Lord Jesus, how He said"—

"All power is given unto me in heaven and in earth."—Matt. xxviii. 18.

The Supreme Investiture.

WHAT an empire is this! Heaven and earth—the Church militant—the Church triumphant—angels and archangels — saints and seraphs. At His mandate the billows were hushed—demons crouched in terror—the grave yielded its prey! "Upon his head are many crowns." He is made "head over *all things* to His Church." Yes! over *all things*, from the minutest to the mightiest. He holds the stars in His right hand.—he walks in the midst of the seven golden candlesticks, feeding every candlestick with the oil of His grace, and preserving every star in its spiritual orbit. The prince of Darkness has "a power," but, God be praised, it is not an "all power;" *potent*, but not *omnipotent*. Christ holds him in a chain. He hath set bounds that he may not pass over. "Satan," we read in the book of Job, "went out (*Chaldee paraphrase*, 'with a licence') trom the presence of the Lord." He was not allowed even to enter the herd of swine till Christ permitted him. He only "*desired*" to have Peter that he might "sift him;" there was a mightier countervailing agency at hand: "*I* have prayed for thee, that thy faith fail not."

Believer, how often is there nothing but this grace of Jesus between thee and everlasting destruction! Satan's key fitting the lock in thy wayward heart; but a stronger than the strong man barring him out;—the power of the adversary fanning the flame; the Omnipotence of Jesus quenching it. Art thou even now feeling the strength of thy corruptions, the weakness of thy graces, the presence of some outward or inward temptation? Look up to Him who has promised to make His grace sufficient for thee; "all power" is His prerogative; "all-sufficiency in all things" is His promise. It is power, too, in conjunction with tenderness. He who sways the sceptre of universal empire "gently leads" His weak, and weary, and burdened ones:—He who counts the number of the stars, loves to count the number of their sorrows; nothing too great, nothing too insignificant for *Him*. He puts every tear into His bottle. He paves His people's pathway with love!

Blessed Jesus! my everlasting interests cannot be in better or in safer keeping than in Thine. I can exultingly rely on the "*all-power*" of Thy Godhead. I can sweetly rejoice in the *all-sympathy* of Thy Manhood. I can confidently repose in the sure wisdom of Thy dealings. "Sometimes," says one, "we expect the blessing in *our* way; He chooses to bestow it in *His.*" But His way and His will must be the best. Infinite love, infinite power, infinite wisdom, are surely infallible guarantees. His purposes nothing can alter. His promises never fail. His word never falls to the ground.

"HEAVEN AND EARTH SHALL PASS AWAY, BUT **MY WORDS** SHALL NOT PASS AWAY."

21st Day.

"Remember the words of the Lord Jesus, how He said"—

"He shall glorify me: for He shall receive of mine, and shall show it unto you."—John xvi. 14.

The Divine Glorifier.

The Holy Spirit glorifying Jesus in the unfoldings of His person, and character, and work, to His people! The great ministering agent between the Church on earth and its glorified Head in Heaven,—carrying up to the Intercessor on the throne, the ever-recurring wants and trials, the perplexities and sins, of believers; and receiving out of His inexhaustible treasury of love,—comfort for their sorrows—strength for their weakness—sympathy for their tears—fulness for their emptiness,—and *this* the one sublime end and object of His gracious agency,—"*He shall glorify Me.*" "He shall not speak of Himself, but whatsoever He shall hear, that shall He speak." My words of sympathy—My omnipotent pleadings—the tender messages sent from an unchanged Human Heart,—all these shall He speak. "He shall tell you," says an old divine, commenting on this passage, "He shall tell you nothing but stories of My love" (*Goodwin*). He will have an ineffable delight in magnifying Me in the affections of My Church and people, and endearing Me to their hearts; and He is all worthy of credence, for He is "the Spirit of truth."

How faithful has He been in every age to this His great office as "the glorifier of Jesus!" See the first manifestation of His power in the Christian Church at the day of Pentecost. What was the grand truth which forms the focus-point of interest in that unparalleled scene, and which brings three thousand stricken penitents to their knees? *It is the Spirit's unfolding of Jesus*—glorifying *Him* in eyes that before saw in

Him no beauty? Hear the key-note of that wondrous sermon, preached "in demonstration of the Spirit, and with power,"—"HIM hath God exalted to be a Prince and a Saviour, to give repentance to His people, and forgiveness of sins."

Ah? it is still the same peerless truth which the Spirit delights to unfold to the stricken sinner, and, in unfolding it, to make it mighty to the pulling down of strongholds. All these glorious inner beauties of Christ's work and character are undiscerned and undiscernible by the natural eye. "It is the Spirit that quickeneth." "No man can call Jesus Lord, but by the Holy Ghost." He is the great Forerunner—a mightier than the Baptist—proclaiming, "Behold the Lamb of God!"

Reader! any bright and realising view you have had of the Saviour's glory and excellency, is of the Spirit's imparting. When in some hour of sorrow you have been led to cleave with pre-eminent consolation to the thought of the Redeemer's exalted sympathy—His dying, ever-living love; or in the hour of death, when you feel the sustaining power of His exceeding great and precious promises;—what is this, but the Holy Spirit, in fulfilment of His all-gracious office, taking of all things of Christ, and showing them unto you; thus enabling you to magnify Him in your body, whether it be by life or death? As your motto should ever be, "*None* BUT *Christ*," and your ever-increasing aspiration, "*More* OF *Christ*," seek to bear in mind who it is that is alone qualified to impart the "excellency of this knowledge."

"THE SPIRIT OF TRUTH WHICH PROCEEDETH FROM THE FATHER, HE SHALL TESTIFY OF ME."

22D DAY.

"Remember the words of the Lord Jesus, how He said"—

"Your sorrow shall be turned into joy."—John xvi. 20.

The Joyful Transformation.

CHRIST'S people are a sorrowing people! Chastisement is their badge—"great tribulation" is their appointed discipline. When they enter the gates of glory, He is represented as wiping away tears from their eyes. But, weeping ones, be comforted! Your Lord's special mission to earth—the great errand He came from heaven to fulfil, was "to bind up the broken-hearted." Your trials are meted out by a tender hand. He *knows* you too well—He *loves* you too well—to make this world tearless and sorrowless! "There must be rain, and hail, and storm," says Rutherford, "in the saint's cloud." Were your earthly course strewed with flowers, and nothing but sunbeams played around your dwelling, it would lead you to forget your *nomadic* life,—that you are but a sojourner here. The tent must at times be struck, pin by pin of the moveable tabernacle taken down, to enable you to say and to feel in the spirit of a pilgrim, "I desire a better country." Meantime, while sorrow is your portion, think of Him who says, "I know your sorrows." Angels cannot say so — they cannot sympathise with you, for trial is a strange word to them. But there is a mightier than they who *can.* All He sends you and appoints you is in love. There is a provision and condition wrapt up in the bosom of every affliction, "*if need be;*" coming from His hand, sorrows and riches are to His people convertible terms. If tempted to murmur at their trials, they are often murmuring at disguised mercies. "Why do you ask me," said Simeon, on his death-bed, "what I *like?* I am the Lord's patient—I cannot but like *everything.*"

And *then*—"your sorrow shall be turned into joy." "The morning cometh"—that bright morning when the dew-drops collected during earth's night of weeping shall sparkle in its beams; when in one blessed *moment* a lifelong experience of trial will be effaced and forgotten, or remembered only by contrast, to enhance the fulness of the joys of immortality. What a revelation of gladness! The map of time disclosed, and every little rill of sorrow, every river will be seen to have been flowing heavenwards, — every rough blast to have been sending the bark nearer the haven! In that jòy, God Himself will participate. In the last "words of Jesus" to His people when they are standing by the triumphal archway of Glory, ready to enter on their thrones and crowns, He speaks of their joy as if it were all *His own.* "Enter ye into the joy *of your Lord.*"

Reader, may this joy be yours! Sit loose to the world's joys. Have a feeling of chastened gratitude and thankfulness when you have them; but beware of resting in them, or investing them with a permanency they cannot have. Jesus had his eye on *heaven* when he added—

"YOUR JOY NO MAN TAKETH FROM YOU."

23D DAY.

"Remember the words of the Lord Jesus, how He said"—

"Father, I will that they also whom thou hast given me, be with me where I am; that they may behold my glory."—John xvii. 24.

The Omnipotent Prayer.

THIS is not the petition of a suppliant, but the claim of a conqueror. There was only *one* request He ever made, or ever *can* make, that was refused; it was the prayer wrung forth by the presence and power of superhuman anguish: "Father, *if it be possible*, let this cup pass from me!" Had that prayer been answered, never could one consolatory "word of Jesus" have been ours. "*If it be possible;*"—*but* for that gracious parenthesis, we must have been lost for ever! In unmurmuring submission, the bitter cup *was* drained; all the dread penalties of the law were borne, the atonement completed, an all-perfect righteousness wrought out; and now, as the stipulated reward of His obedience and sufferings, the Victor claims His trophies. What are they? Those that were given Him of the Father—the countless multitudes redeemed by His blood. These He "*wills*" to be with Him "where He is"—the spectators of His glory, and partakers of His crown. Wondrous word and will of a dying testator! His last prayer on earth is an importunate pleading for their glorification; His parting wish is to meet them in heaven: as if these earthly jewels were needed to make His crown complete,—their happiness and joy the needful complement of His own!

Reader! learn from this, the grand element in the bliss of your future condition—it is *the presence of Christ;* "*with Me* where I am." It matters comparatively little as to the locality of heaven. "We shall see *Him* as He is," is "the blessed hope" of the Christian.

Heaven would be *no* heaven without Jesus; the withdrawal of His presence would be like the blotting out of the sun from the firmament; it would uncrown every seraph, and unstring every harp. But, blessed thought! it is His own stipulation in His testamentary prayer, that Eternity is to be spent in union and communion with *Himself*, gazing on the unfathomed mysteries of His love, becoming more assimilated to His glorious image, and drinking deeper from the ocean of His own joy.

If anything can enhance the magnitude of this promised bliss, it is the concluding words of the verse, in which He grounds His plea for its bestowment: "*I will*—that they behold my glory;"—why? "For Thou lovedst (not *them*, but) ME before the foundation of the world!" It is equivalent to saying, "If Thou wouldst give *Me* a continued proof of Thine everlasting love and favour to Myself, it is by loving and exalting My redeemed people. In loving *them* and glorifying them, Thou art loving and glorifying Me: so endearingly are their interests and My own bound up together!"

Believer, think of that all-prevailing voice, at this moment pleading for thee within the veil!—that omnipotent "*Father, I will*," securing every needed boon! There is given, so to speak, a blank *cheque* by which He and His people may draw indefinite supplies out of the exhaustless treasury of the Father's grace and love. God Himself endorses it with the words, "Son, Thou art ever with me, and all that I have is Thine." How it would reconcile us to Earth's bitterest sorrows, and hallow Earth's holiest joys, if we saw them thus hanging on the "*will*" of an all-wise Intercessor, who ever pleads in love, and never pleads in vain!

"BE IT UNTO ME ACCORDING TO THY WORD."

24TH DAY.

"Remember the words of the Lord Jesus, how He said"—

"Because I live, ye shall live also."—John xiv. 19."

The Immutable Pledge. GOD sometimes selects the most stable and enduring objects in the material world to illustrate His unchanging faithfulness and love to His Church. "As the mountains are round about Jerusalem, so doth the Lord compass his people." But here, the Redeemer fetches an argument from *His own everlasting nature.* He stakes, so to speak, His own existence on that of His saints. "*Because I live,* ye shall live also."

Believer! read in this "word of Jesus" thy glorious title-deed. *Thy Saviour lives*—and His life is the guarantee of thine own. Our true Joseph is alive. "He is our Brother. He talks kindly to us!" That life of His, is all that is between us and everlasting ruin. But with Christ for our life, how inviolable our security! The great Fountain of being must first be dried up, before the streamlet can. The great Sun must first be quenched, ere one glimmering satellite which He lights up with His splendour can. Satan must first pluck the crown from that glorified Head, before he can touch one jewel in the crown of His people. They cannot shake one pillar without shaking first the throne. "If we perish," says Luther, "Christ perisheth with us."

Reader! is thy life now "hid with Christ in God?" Dost thou know the blessedness of a vital and living union with a living, life-giving Saviour? Canst thou say with humble and joyous confidence, amid the fitfulness of thine own ever-changing frames and feelings, "Nevertheless I live, yet not I, but Christ liveth in me?" "*Jesus liveth!*"—They are the happiest words a lost soul and a lost world can hear! Job, four thousand years ago, rejoiced in them. "I know," says he, "that I have *a living Kinsman.*" John, in his Patmos exile, rejoiced in them. "I am He that liveth" (or *the Living One*), was the simple but sublime utterance with which he was addressed by that same "Kinsman," when He appeared arrayed in the lustres of His glorified humanity. "This is *the* record" (as if there was a whole gospel comprised in the statement), "that God hath given to us eternal life, and this *life* is in His Son." St. Paul, in the 8th chapter to the Romans—that finest portraiture of Christian character and privilege ever drawn, begins with "no condemnation," and ends with "no separation." Why "no separation?" Because the life of the believer is incorporated with that of his adorable Head and Surety. The colossal Heart of redeemed humanity beats upon the throne, sending its mighty pulsations through every member of His body; so that, before the believer's spiritual life can be destroyed, Omnipotence must become feebleness, and Immutability become mutable!

But, blessed Jesus, "Thy word is very sure, therefore Thy servant loveth it."

"I GIVE UNTO THEM ETERNAL LIFE, AND THEY SHALL NEVER PERISH, NEITHER SHALL ANY MAN PLUCK THEM OUT OF MY HAND."

25TH DAY.

"Remember the words of the Lord Jesus, how He said"—

"Lo, I am with you alway, even unto the end of the world."—Matt. xxviii. 20.

The Abiding Presence.

SUCH were "the words of Jesus" when He was just about to ascend to Heaven. The mediatorial throne was in view—the harps of glory were sounding in His ears; but all His thoughts are on the pilgrim Church He is to leave behind. His last words and benedictions are for *them*. "I go," He seems to say, "to Heaven, to my purchased crown—to the fellowship of angels—to the presence of my Father; *but*, nevertheless, 'Lo! I am with *you* alway, even unto the end of the world.'"

How faithfully did the Apostles, to whom this promise was first addressed, experience its reality! Hear the testimony of the beloved disciple who had once leant on his Divine Master's bosom —who "had heard, and seen, and looked upon Him." That glorified bosom was now hid from his sight; but does he speak of an absent Lord, and of His fellowship only as among the holy memories of the past? No! with rejoicing emphasis he can exclaim—"Truly our fellowship IS with .... *Jesus Christ.*"

Amid so much that is fugitive here, how the heart clings to this assurance of the abiding presence of the Saviour! Our best earthly friends—a few weeks may estrange them;—centuries have rolled on—Christ is still the same. How blessed to think, that if I am indeed a child of God, there is not the lonely instant I am without His guardianship! When the beams of the morning visit my chamber, the brighter beams of a brighter Sun are shining upon me. When the shadows of evening are gathering around, "it is not night, if He, the unsetting 'Sun of my soul,' is near." His is no fitful companionship—present in prosperity, gone in adversity. He never changes. He is always the same,—in sickness and solitude, in joy and in sorrow, in life and in death. Not more faithfully did the pillar-cloud and column of fire of old precede Israel, till the last murmuring ripple of Jordan fell on their ears on the shores of Canaan, than does the presence and love of Jesus abide with His people. Has His word of promise ever proved false? Let the great cloud of witnesses now in glory testify. "Not one thing hath failed of all that the Lord our God hath spoken." *This* "word of the Lord is tried"—"having loved His own, which were in the world, He loved them *unto the end.*"

Believer! art thou troubled and tempted? Do dark providences and severe afflictions seem to belie the truth and reality of this gracious assurance? Art thou ready, with Gideon, to say,

"If the Lord be indeed with us, why has all this befallen us?" Be assured He has some faithful end in view. By the removal of prized and cherished earthly props and refuges, He would unfold more of his own tenderness. Amid the wreck and ruin of earthly joys, which, it may be, the grave has hidden from your sight, One nearer, dearer, tenderer still, would have you say of Himself, "*The Lord liveth;* and blessed be my Rock; and let the God of my salvation be exalted." "Thanks be to God, who *always* maketh us to triumph in Christ." Yes! and never more so than when, stripped of all competing objects of creature affection, we are left, like the disciples on the mount, with "*Jesus only!*"

"THESE THINGS HAVE I SPOKEN UNTO YOU, THAT IN ME YE MIGHT HAVE PEACE."

26TH DAY.

"Remember the words of the Lord Jesus, how He said"—

"I am the resurrection and the life: he that believeth in me, though he were dead, yet he shall live."—John. xi. 25.

The Resurrection and Life.

WHAT a voice is this breaking over a world which for six thousand years has been a dormitory of sin and death! For four thousand of these years, heathendom could descry no light through the bars of the grave; her oracles were dumb on the great doctrine of a future state, and more especially regarding the body's resurrection. Even the Jewish Church, under the Old Testament dispensation, seemed to enjoy little more than fitful and uncertain glimmerings, like men groping in the dark. It required death's great Abolisher to show, to a benighted world, the luminous "path of life." With Him rested the "bringing in of a better hope"—the unfolding of "the mystery which had been hid from ages and generations." Marvellous disclosure! that this mortal frame, decomposed and resolved into its original dust, shall yet start from its ashes, remodelled and reconstructed—"a glorified body!" Not like "the earthly tabernacle" (a mere shifting and moveable *tent*, as the word denotes), but incorruptible—immortal! The beauteous transformation of the insect from its chrysalis state—the buried seed springing up from its tiny grave to the full-eared corn or gorgeous flower—these are nature's mute utterances as to the possibility of this great truth, which required the unfoldings of "a more sure word of prophecy." But the Gospel has fully revealed what Reason, in her loftiest imaginings, could not have dreamt of. Jesus "hath brought life and immortality to light." He, the Bright and Morning Star, hath "turned the shadow of death into the morning." He gives, in His own resurrection, the earnest of that of His people;—He is the first-fruits of the immortal harvest yet to be gathered into the garner of Heaven.

Precious truth! This "word of Jesus" spans like a celestial rainbow the entrance to the dark valley. Death is robbed of its sting. In the case of every child of God, the grave holds in custody precious, because redeemed, dust. Talk of it not, as being committed to a dishonoured tomb!—it is locked up, rather, in the casket, of God until the day "when He maketh up His jewels," when it will be fashioned in deathless beauty like unto the glorified body of the Redeemer. Angels, meanwhile, are commissioned to keep watch over it, till the trump of the archangel shall proclaim the great "Easter of creation." They are the "reapers," waiting for the world's great "Harvest Home," when Jesus Himself shall come again—not as He once did, humiliated and in sorrow, but rejoicing in the thought of bringing back all His sheaves with him.

Afflicted and bereaved Christian!—thou who mayest be mourning in bitterness those who are not—rejoice through thy tears in these hopes "full of immortality." The silver cord is only "loosed," not broken. Perchance, as thou standest in the chamber of death, or by the brink of the grave,—in the depths of that awful solitude and silence which reigns around,—this may be thy plaintive and mournful soliloquy—"Shall the dust praise Thee?" Yes, it *shall!* This very dust that hears now unheeded thy footsteps, and unmoved thy tears, shall through eternity praise its redeeming God—it shall proclaim His truth!

"LORD, TO WHOM SHALL WE GO BUT UNTO THEE, THOU HAST THE WORDS OF ETERNAL LIFE."

27TH DAY.

"Remember the words of the Lord Jesus, how He said"—

"A little while, and ye shall not see me; and again, a little while, and ye shall see me, because I go to the Father."—John xvi. 16.

The Little While.

LONG seem the moments when we are separated from the friend we love. An absent brother—how his return is looked and longed for! The "Elder Brother"—the "Living Kinsman"—sends a message to His waiting Church and people—a word of solace, telling that *soon* ("a little while,") and He will be back again, never again to leave them.

There are indeed blessed moments of communion which the believer enjoys with His beloved Lord *now;* but how fitful and transient! To-day, life is a brief Emmaus journey—the soul happy in the presence and love of an unseen Saviour. To-morrow, He is *gone;* and the bereft spirit is led to interrogate itself in plaintive sorrow,—"Where is now thy God?" Even when there is no such experience of darkness and depression, how much there is in the world around to fill the believer with sadness! His Lord rejected and disowned—His love set at nought—His providences slighted—His name blasphemed—His creation groaning and travailing in pain—disunion, too, among His people—His loving heart wounded in the house of His friends!

But "yet a little while," and all this mystery of iniquity will be finished. The absent Brother's footfall will soon be heard,—no longer "as a wayfaring man who turneth aside to tarry for a night," but to receive His people into the permanent "mansions" His love has been preparing, and from which they shall go no more out. Oh, blessed day! when creation will put on her Easter robes—when her Lord, so long dishonoured, will be enthroned amid the hosannahs of a rejoicing universe—angels lauding Him—saints crowning Him—sin, the dark plague-spot on His universe, extinguished for ever—death swallowed up in eternal victory!

And it is but "a little while!" "Yet a little while," we elsewhere read, "and He that shall come, will come, and will not tarry" (literally, "a little while as may be.") "He will stay not a moment longer," says Goodwin, "than He hath despatched all our business in Heaven for us." With what joy will He send His mission-Angel with the announcement, "the little while is at an end;" and to issue the invitation to the great festival of glory, "Come! for all things are ready!"

Child of sorrow! think often of this "*little while.*" "The days of thy mourning will soon be ended." There is a limit set to thy suffering time,—"After that ye have suffered a WHILE."

Every wave is numbered between you and the haven; and then when that haven is reached, oh, what an apocalypse of glory!—the "little while" of time merged into the great and unending "while of eternity!—to be *for ever with the Lord*—the same unchanged and unchanging Saviour!

"A little while, and ye *shall* see me!" Would that the eye of faith might be kept more intently fixed on "that glorious appearing!" How the world, with its guilty fascinations, tries to dim and obscure this blessed hope! How the heart is prone to throw out its fibres here, and get them rooted in some perishable object! Reader! seek to dwell more habitually on this the grand consummation of all thy dearest wishes. "Stand on the edge of your nest, pluming your wings for flight." Like the mother of Sisera, be looking for the expected chariot.

"HE IS FAITHFUL THAT PROMISED."

28TH DAY.

"Remember the words of the Lord Jesus, how He said"—

"Blessed are the pure in heart, for they shall see God."— Mat. v. 8.

The Beatific Vision.

HERE is HEAVEN! This "word of Jesus" represents the future state of the glorified to consist not in locality, but in character; the essence of its bliss is the full vision and fruition of God. Our attention is called from all vague and indefinite theories about the *circumstantials* of future happiness. The one grand object of contemplation—the "glory which excelleth," is *the sight of God Himself!* The one grand practical lesson enforced on His people, is the cultivation of that purity of heart without which none could *see*, or (even could we suppose it possible to be admitted to *see* Him) none could *enjoy* God! "The kingdom of Heaven cometh not with observation . . . the kingdom of God is *within* you."

Reader, hast thou attained any of this heart-purity and heart-preparation? It has been beautifully said that "the openings of the streets of heaven are on earth." Even here we may enjoy, in the possession of holiness, some foretaste of coming bliss. Who has not felt that the happiest moments of their lives were those of close walking with God—nearness to the mercy-seat—when self was surrendered, and the eye was directed to the glory of Jesus, with most single, unwavering, undivided aim? What will Heaven be, but the entire surrender of the soul to Him, without any bias to evil, without the fear of corruption within echoing to temptation without; every thought brought into captivity to the obedience of Christ; no contrariety to His mind; all in blessed unison with His will; the whole *being* impregnated with holiness—the intellect purified and ennobled, consecrating all its powers to His service—memory, a holy repository of pure and hallowed recollections—the affections, without one competing rival, purged from all the dross of earthliness—the love of God, the one supreme animating passion—the glory of God, the motive principle interfused through every thought, and feeling, and action of the life immortal; in one word, the heart a pellucid fountain; no sediment to dim its purity, "no angel of sorrow" to come and trouble the pool! The long night of life over, and *this* the glory of the eternal morrow which succeeds it! "I shall be satisfied when I awake, with *Thy* likeness."

Yes, this is Heaven, subjectively and objectively—*purity of heart* and "*God all in all!*" Much, doubtless, there may and will be of a subordinate kind, to intensify the bliss of the redeemed; communion with saints and angels;

re-admission into the society of death-divided friends: but all these will fade before the great central glory, "God Himself shall be with them, and be their God; they shall *see His face!*" Believers have been aptly called *heliotropes*—turning their faces as the sunflower towards the Sun of Righteousness, and hanging their leaves in sadness and sorrow, when that Sun is away. It will be in heaven the emblem is complete. *There*, every flower in the heavenly garden will be turned Godwards, bathing its tints of loveliness in the glory that excelleth! Reader, may it be yours, when o'er-canopied by that cloudless sky, to know all the marvels contained in these few glowing words, "We shall be like Him, for we shall see him as He is."

"AND EVERY MAN THAT HATH THIS HOPE IN HIM PURIFIETH HIMSELF EVEN AS HE IS PURE."

29TH DAY.

"Remember the words of the Lord Jesus, how He said"—

"In my Father's house are many mansions."—John xiv. 2.

The Many Mansions.

WHAT a home aspect there is in this "word of Jesus!" He comforts His Church by telling them that soon their wilderness-wanderings will be finished,—the tented tabernacle suited to their present probation-state exchanged for the enduring "mansion!" Nor will it be any strange dwelling: a *Father's* home—a *Father's* welcome awaits them. There will be accommodation for all. Thousands have already entered its shining gates,—patriarchs, prophets, saints, martyrs, young and old, and still there is room!

The pilgrim's motto on earth is, "Here we have no continuing city." Even "Sabbath tents" must be struck. Holy seasons of communion must terminate. "Arise, let us go hence!" is a summons which disturbs the sweetest moments of tranquillity in the Church below; but *in Heaven*, every believer becomes a pillar in the temple of God, and "he shall *go no more out*." Here it is but the lodging of a wayfarer turning aside to tarry for the brief night of earth. Here we are but "tenants at will;" our possessions are but moveables—ours to-day, gone to-morrow. But these many "mansions" are an inheritance incorruptible and unfading. Nothing can touch the heavenly patrimony. Once within the Father's house, and we are in the house for ever!

Think, too, of Jesus, gone to *prepare* these mansions,—"I go to prepare a place for you." What a wondrous thought—Jesus now busied in Heaven in His Church's behalf! He can find no abode in all His wide dominions, befitting as a permanent dwelling for His ransomed ones. He says, "I will make new heavens and a new earth. I will found a special kingdom—I will rear eternal mansions expressly for those I have redeemed with my blood!"

Reader, let the prospect of a dwelling in this "house of the Lord for ever," reconcile thee to any of the roughnesses or difficulties in thy present path—to thy pilgrim provision and pilgrim fare. Let the distant beacon-light, that so cheeringly speaks of a *Home* brighter and better far than the happiest of earthly ones, lead thee to forget the intervening billows, or to think of them only as wafting thee nearer and nearer to thy desired haven! "Would," says a saint, who has now entered on his rest, "that one could read, and write, and pray, and eat and drink, and compose one's self to sleep, as with the thought,—soon to be in heaven, and that for ever and ever!"

"My Father's house!" How many a departing spirit has been cheered and consoled by the sight of these glorious Mansions looming through the mists of the dark valley,—the tears of weeping friends rebuked by the gentle chiding—"If ye loved me, ye would rejoice, because I said, I go unto *my Father!*" Death truly is but the entrance to this our Father's house. We speak of the "*shadow of death*"—it is only the shadow which falls on the portico as we stand for a moment knocking at the longed-for gate—the next! a Father's voice of welcome is heard—

"SON! THOU ART EVER WITH ME, AND ALL THAT I HAVE IS THINE."

80TH DAY.

"Remember the words of the Lord Jesus, how He said"—

"I will come again, and receive you unto myself; that where I am, there ye may be also."—John xiv. 8.

The Promised Return.

ANOTHER "word of promise" concerning the Church's "blessed hope." Orphaned pilgrims, dry your tears! Soon the Morning Hour will strike, and the sighs of a groaning and burdened creation be heard no more. Earth's six thousand years of toil and sorrow are waning; the Millennial Sabbath is at hand. Jesus will soon be heard to repeat concerning all his sleeping saints, what He said of old regarding one of them: "I go to awake them out of sleep!" Your beloved Lord's first coming was in humiliation and woe; His name was—the "Man of Sorrows;" He had to travel on, amid darkness and desertion, His blood-stained path; a chaplet of thorns was the only crown He bore. But soon He will come "the second time without a sin-offering unto salvation," never again to leave His Church, but to receive those who followed Him in His cross, to be everlasting partakers with Him in His crown. He may seem to tarry. External nature, in her unvarying and undeviating sequences, gives no indication of His approach. Centuries have elapsed since He uttered the promise, and still He lingers; the everlasting hills wear no streak of approaching dawn; we seem to listen in vain for the noise of His chariot wheels. "But the Lord is not slack concerning His promise;" He gives you "this word" in addition to many others as a *keepsake*—a pledge and guarantee for the certainty of His return,—"*I will come again.*"

Who can conceive all the surpassing blessedness connected with that advent? The Elder Brother arrived to fetch the younger brethren home!—the true Joseph revealing Himself in unutterable tenderness to the brethren who were once estranged from Him—"receiving them unto himself"—not satisfied with apportioning a kingdom for them, but, as if all His own joy and bliss were intermingled with theirs, "Where *I am*," says He, "there *you* must be also." "Him that overcometh," says He again, "will I grant to sit with Me on My Throne."

Believer, can you *now* say with some of the holy transport of the apostle, "Whom having not seen, we love?" What must it be when you come to see Him "face to face," and that for ever and ever! If you can tell of precious hours of communion in a sin-striken, woe-worn world, with a treacherous heart, and an imperfect or divided love, what must it be when you come, in a sinless, sorrowless state, with purified and renewed affections, to see the King in His beauty! The letter of an absent brother, cheering and consolatory as it is, is a poor compensation for the joys of personal and visible communion. The absent Elder Brother on the Throne speaks to you *now* only by His Word and Spirit,—soon you shall be admitted to His immediate fellowship, seeing him "as He is"—He Himself unfolding the wondrous chart of His providence and grace—leading you about from fountain to fountain among the living waters, and with his own gentle hand wiping the last lingering tear-drop from your eye. *Heaven an everlasting home with Jesus!* "Where I am, there ye may be also."—He has appended a cheering postscript to this word, on which He has "caused us to hope:"—

"HE WHICH TESTIFIETH THESE THINGS SAITH, SURELY I COME QUICKLY."

31st Day.

"Remember the words of the Lord Jesus, how He said"—

"Blessed are those servants whom the Lord when He cometh shall find watching."—Luke xii. 37.

The Closing Benediction.

Child of God! is this thine attitude, as the expectant of thy Lord's appearing? Are thy loins girded, and thy lights burning? If the cry were to break upon thine ears this day, "Behold the Bridegroom cometh," couldst thou joyfully respond—"Lo, this is my God, I have waited for him?" When He may come, we cannot tell;—ages may elapse before *then*. It may be centuries before our graves are gilded with the beams of a Millennial sun; but while He *may* or may *not* come *soon*, He *must* come at some time—ay, and the day of our death is virtually to all of us the day of His coming.

Reader! put not off the solemn preparation. Be not deceived or deluded with the mocker's presumptuous challenge, "Where is the promise of His coming?" See to it that the calls of an engrossing world without, do not foster this procrastinating spirit within. It may be now or never with thee. Put not off thy sowing time till harvest time. Leave nothing for a dying hour, *but to die*, and calmly to resign thy spirit into the hands of Jesus. Of all times, *that* is the least suitable to have the vessel plenished—to attend to the great business of life when life is ebbing—to trim the lamp when the oil is done and it is flickering in its socket—to begin to watch, when the summons is heard to leave the watch-tower to meet our God!

Were you never struck how often, amid the many *gentle* words of Jesus, the summons "to watch," is over and over repeated, like a succession of alarum-bells breaking ever and anon, amid chimes of heavenly music, to rouse a sleeping Church and a slumbering world?

Let this last "Word" of thy Lord's send thee to thy knees with the question,—"Am I indeed a servant of Christ?" Have I fled to Him, and am I reposing in Him, as my only Saviour?—or am I still lingering, like Lot, when I should be escaping—sleeping, when I should be waking—neglecting and trifling, when "a long eternity is lying at my door?" He is my last and only refuge; neglect Him—*all is lost!*

Believer! thou who art standing on thy watch-tower, be more faithful than ever at thy post. Remember what is implied in watching. It is no dreamy state of inactive torpor: it is a holy jealousy over the heart—wakeful vigilance regarding sin—every avenue and loophole of the soul carefully guarded. *Holy living* is the best, the *only*, preparative for *holy dying*. "Persuade yourself," says Rutherford, "the King is coming. Read His letter sent before Him, 'Behold I come quickly;' wait with the wearied night-watch for the breaking of the Eastern sky."

Let these "*Words of Jesus*" we have now been meditating upon in this little volume, be as the Golden Bells of old, hung on the vestments of the officiating High Priest, emitting sweet sounds to His spiritual Israel—telling that the *true High Priest* is still living and pleading in "the Holiest of all;" and that soon He will come forth to pour His blessing on His waiting Church. We have been pleasingly employed in gathering up a few "crumbs" falling from "the Master's table." Soon we shall have, not the "*Words*" but the *presence* of Jesus—not the crumbs falling from His table, but everlasting fellowship with the Master Himself.

"AMEN, EVEN SO, COME, LORD JESUS."

"Wherefore

Comfort One Another

with

THESE WORDS."

---

1 Thess. iv. 18.

THE

FAITHFUL PROMISER.

BY THE AUTHOR OF

"THE WORDS OF JESUS," "THE MORNING AND NIGHT WATCHES," ETC.

"Whereby are given unto us exceeding great and precious promises."—2 PET. i. 4.

NEW YORK:
STANFORD & DELISSER,
No. 508, BROADWAY.
1858.

The
Faithful Promiser.

It has often been felt a delightful exercise by the child of God, to take, night by night, an individual promise and plead it at the mercy-seat. Often are our prayers *pointless*, from not following, in this respect, the example of the sweet Psalmist of Israel, the Royal Promise pleader, who delighted to direct his finger to some particular "word" of the Faithful Promiser, saying, "Remember Thy word unto Thy servant, on which thou hast caused me to hope!"

The following are a few gleanings from the Promise Treasury,—a few crumbs from "the Master's Table," which may serve to help the thoughts in the hour of closet meditation, or the season of sorrow.

ST. M——,
December, 1849.

1ST DAY OF MONTH.

"He is Faithful that Promised."

"Come now, let us reason together, saith the Lord: Though your sins be as scarlet, they shall be as white as snow; though they be red like crimson, they shall be as wool."—ISAIAH i. 18.

Pardoning Grace.

MY soul! thy God summons thee to His audience chamber! Infinite purity seeks to reason with infinite vileness! Deity stoops to speak to dust! Dread not the meeting. It is the most gracious, as well as wondrous of all conferences. Jehovah himself breaks silence! He utters the best tidings a lost soul or a lost world can hear: "God is in Christ reconciling the world unto Himself, not imputing unto men their trespasses." What! *Scarlet* sins, and *crimson* sins! and these all to be forgiven and forgotten! The just God "justifying" the unjust!—the mightiest of all beings, the kindest of all! Oh! what is there in thee to merit such love as this? Thou mightest have known thy God only as the "consuming fire," and had nothing before thee save "a fearful looking for of vengeance!" This gracious conference bids thee dispel thy fears! It tells thee it is no longer a "fearful," but a *blessed* thing to fall into His hands? Hast thou closed with these His overtures? Until thou art at peace with Him, happiness must be a stranger to thy bosom. Though thou hast all else beside, bereft of God thou must be "bereft indeed." Lord! I come! As thy pardoning grace is freely tendered, so shall I freely accept it. May it be mine, even now, to listen to the gladdening accents, "Son! Daughter! be of good cheer! thy sins, which are many, are all forgiven thee."

"REMEMBER *THIS* WORD UNTO THY SERVANT, UPON WHICH THOU HAST CAUSED ME TO HOPE!"

2D DAY.

"He is Faithful that Promised."

"As thy days, so shall thy strength be."—DEUT. xxxiii. 25.

Needful Grace. GOD does not give grace till the hour of trial comes. But when it *does* come, the amount of grace, and the nature of the special grace required is vouchsafed. My soul, do not dwell with painful apprehension on the future. Do not anticipate coming sorrows; perplexing thyself with the grace needed for future emergencies; to-morrow will bring its promised grace along with to-morrow's trials. God, wishing to keep His people humble, and dependent on himself, gives not a stock of grace; He metes it out for every day's exigencies, that they may be constantly "travelling between their own emptiness and Christ's fulness"—their own weakness and Christ's strength. But *when* the exigency comes, thou mayest safely trust an

Almighty arm to bear thee through! Is there now some "thorn in the flesh" sent to lacerate thee? Thou mayest have been entreating the Lord for its removal. Thy prayer has, doubtless, been heard and answered; but not in the way, perhaps, expected or desired by thee. The "thorn" may still be left to goad, the trial may still be left to buffet; but "more grace" has been given to endure them. Oh! how often have His people thus been led to glory in their infirmities and triumph in their afflictions, seeing the power of Christ rests more abundantly upon them! The strength which the hour of trial brings, often makes the Christian a wonder to himself!

"REMEMBER *THIS* WORD UNTO THY SERVANT, UPON WHICH THOU HAST CAUSED ME TO HOPE!"

3D DAY.

"He is Faithful that Promised."

"God is able to make all grace abound toward you; that ye, always having all sufficiency in all things, may abound to every good work."—2 COR. ix. 8.

All-Sufficient Grace.

"ALL-SUFFICIENCY in all things!" Believer! surely thou art "thoroughly furnished!" Grace is no scanty thing, doled out in pittances. It is a glorious treasury, which the key of prayer can always unlock, but never empty. A fountain, "full, flowing, *ever* flowing, *over*flowing." Mark these three ALL's in this precious promise. It is a threefold link in a golden chain, let down from a throne of grace by a God of grace. "*All-grace!*"—"*all-sufficiency!*" in "*all things!*" and these to "abound." Oh! precious thought! My want cannot impoverish that inexhaustible treasury of grace! Myriads are hourly hanging on it, and drawing from it, and yet there is no diminution: "Out of that fulness all we too may receive, and grace for grace!" My soul, dost not thou love to dwell on that all-abounding grace? Thine own insufficiency in every thing, met with an "all-sufficiency in all things!" Grace in all circumstances and situations, in all vicissitudes and changes, in all the varied phases of the Christian's being. Grace in sunshine and storm—in health and in sickness—in life and in death. Grace for the old believer and the young believer, the tried believer, and the weak believer, and the tempted believer. Grace *for* duty, and grace *in* duty,—grace to carry the joyous cup with a steady hand,—grace to drink the bitter cup with an unmurmuring spirit,—grace to have prosperity sanctified,—grace to say, through tears, "Thy will be done!"

"REMEMBER *THIS* WORD UNTO THY SERVANT, UPON WHICH THOU HAST CAUSED ME TO HOPE.!"

4TH DAY.

"He is Faithful that Promised."

"I will not leave you comfortless; I will come to you."—JOHN xiv. 18.

Comforting Grace.

BLESSED Jesus! How thy presence sanctifies trial, takes loneliness from the chamber of sickness, and the sting from the chamber of death! Bright and Morning Star! precious at all times, thou art never *so* precious as in "the dark and cloudy day!" The bitterness of sorrow is well worth enduring to have thy promised consolations. How well qualified, thou Man of Sorrows, to be my Comforter! How well fitted to dry my tears, Thou who didst shed so many thyself! What are *my* tears—my sorrows—my crosses—my losses, compared with Thine, who didst shed first Thy tears, and then Thy blood for *me!* Mine are all deserved, and infinitely more than deserved. How different, O Spotless Lamb of God, those pangs which rent Thy guiltless bosom! How sweet those comforts Thou hast promised to the comfortless, when I think of them as flowing from an Almighty *Fellow-Sufferer*,—"A brother born for adversity," —the "Friend that sticketh closer than any brother!"—one who can say, with all the refined sympathies of a holy exalted human nature, "I know your sorrows!" My soul! calm thy griefs! There is not a sorrow thou canst experience, but Jesus, in the treasury of grace, has an exact corresponding solace: "In the multitude of the *sorrows* I have in my heart, Thy *comforts* delight my soul!"

"REMEMBER *THIS* WORD UNTO THY SERVANT, UPON WHICH THOU HAST CAUSED ME TO HOPE!"

5TH DAY.

"He is Faithful that Promised."

"Satan hath desired to have you, that he may sift you as wheat; but I have prayed for thee, that thy faith fail not.—LUKE xxii. 31, 32.

Restraining Grace.

WHAT a scene does this unfold! Satan tempting —Jesus praying! Satan sifting—Jesus pleading! "The strong man assailing"—"the stronger than the strong" beating him back! Believer? here is the past history and present secret of thy safety in the midst of temptation. An interceding Saviour was at thy side, saying to every threatening wave, "Thus far shalt thou go, and no farther?" God often permits His people to be on the very verge of the precipice, to remind them of their own weakness; *but never farther than the verge!* The restraining hand and grace of Omnipotence is ready to rescue them. "Although he fall, yet shall he not be cast down utterly; and why? for the Lord upholdeth him with His right hand!" The wolf may be prowling for his prey; but what can he do when the Shepherd is always there, tending with the watchful eye that "neither slumbers nor sleeps?" Who cannot subscribe to the testimony, "When my foot slipped, Thy mercy, O Lord! held me up?" Who can look back on his past pilgrimage, and fail to see it crowded with Ebenezers, with this inscription: "Thou hast delivered my soul from death, mine eyes from tears, and my feet from falling?" My soul, where wouldst thou have been this day, hadst thou not been "*kept*" by the power of God?

"REMEMBER *THIS* WORD UNTO THY SERVANT, UPON WHICH THOU HAST CAUSED ME TO HOPE!"

6TH DAY.

"He is Faithful that Promised."

"I will heal their backsliding."—HOSEA xiv. 4.

Restoring Grace.

WANDERING again! And has He not left me to perish? Stumbling and straying on the dark mountains, away from the Shepherd's eye and the Shepherd's fold, shall He not leave the erring wanderer to the fruit of his own ways, and his truant heart to go hopelessly onward in its career of guilty estrangement? "My thoughts," says God, "are not as your thoughts, neither are your ways my ways." Man would say, "Go, perish! ungrateful apostate!" God says, "Return, ye backsliding children!" The Shepherd *will* not, *cannot* suffer the sheep to perish He has purchased with His own blood. How wondrous His forbearance towards it! —tracking its guilty steps, and ceasing not the pursuit till He lays the wanderer on His shoulders, and returns with it to His fold rejoicing! My soul! why increase by farther departures thine own distance from the fold? —why lengthen the dreary road thy gracious Shepherd has to traverse in bringing thee back? Delay not thy return! Provoke no longer His patience; venture no farther on forbidden ground. He waits with outstretched arms to welcome thee once more to His bosom. Be humble for the past, trust Him for the future. Think of thy former backslidings, and tremble; think of His forbearance, and be filled with holy gratitude; think of His promised grace, "and take courage."

"REMEMBER *THIS* WORD UNTO THY SERVANT, UPON WHICH THOU HAST CAUSED ME TO HOPE!"

7TH DAY.

"He is Faithful that Promised."

"He which hath begun a good work in you, will perform it until the day of Jesus Christ.—PHIL. i. 6.

Sanctifying Grace.

READER! is the good work begun in thee? Art thou holy? Is sin crucifying? Are thy heart's idols, one by one abolished? Is the world less to thee, and eternity more to thee? Is more of thy Saviour's image impressed on thy character, and thy Saviour's love more enthroned in thy heart? Is "Salvation" to thee more "the one thing needful?" Oh! take heed! there can be no middle ground, no standing still; or if it be so, thy position must be a false one. The Saviour's blood is not more necessary to give thee a title to Heaven, than His Spirit to give thee a meetness for it. "If any man have not the Spirit of Christ, he is *none of His!*" "Onwards!" should be thy motto. There is no standing still in the life of faith. "The man," says Augustine, "who says '*Enough*,' that man's soul is lost?" Let this be the superscription in all thy ways and doings, "Holiness to the Lord." Let the monitory word exercise over thee its habitual power, "Without holiness no man shall see the Lord." Moreover, remember, that to be holy, is to be happy. The two are convertible terms. Holiness! It is the secret and spring of the joy of angels; and the more of holiness attained on earth—the nearer and closer my walk is with God—the more of a sweet earnest shall I have of the bliss that awaits me in a holy Heaven. Oh! my soul, let it be thy sacred ambition to "Be holy!"

"REMEMBER *THIS* WORD UNTO THY SERVANT, UPON WHICH THOU HAST CAUSED ME TO HOPE!"

8TH DAY.

"He is Faithful that Promised."

"They that wait upon the Lord shall renew their strength; they shall mount up with wings as eagles; they shall run, and not be weary; they shall walk, and not faint.—ISAIAH xl. 31.

Reviving Grace.

"WILT thou not revive us, O Lord?" My soul! art thou conscious of thy declining state? Is thy walk less with God, thy frame less heavenly? Hast thou less conscious nearness to the mercy-seat,—diminished communion with thy Saviour? Is prayer less a privilege than it has been?—the pulsations of spiritual life more languid, and fitful, and spasmodic?—the bread of life less relished?—the seen, and the temporal, and the tangible, displacing the unseen and eternal? Art thou sinking down into this state of drowsy self-contentment, this conformity-life with the world, forfeiting all the happiness of true religion, and risking and endangering the better life to come? Arise! call upon thy God! "Wilt thou not revive us, O Lord?" He might have returned nothing but the withering repulse, "How often would I have gathered thee; but thou wouldst not!" "Ephraim is joined to his idols; let him alone!" But "in wrath He remembers mercy." "They *shall* revive as the corn." "The mouth of the Lord hath spoken it." How and where is reviving grace to be found? He gives thee, in this precious promise, the key. It is on thy bended *knees*—by a return to thy deserted and unfrequented chamber! "*They that wait upon the Lord!*" "Wait on the Lord; be of good cheer, and He shall strengthen thine heart; wait, I say, on the Lord!"

"REMEMBER *THIS* WORD UNTO THY SERVANT, UPON WHICH THOU HAST CAUSED ME TO HOPE!"

9TH DAY.

"He is Faithful that Promised."

"The righteous shall hold on his way."—JOB xvii. 9.

Persevering Grace.

READER! how comforting to thee amid the ebbings and flowings of thy changing history, to know that the change is all with thee, and not with thy God! Thy spiritual bark may be tossed on waves of temptation, in many a dark midnight. Thou mayest think thy pilot hath left thee, and be ready continually to say, "Where is my God?" But fear not! The bark which bears thy spiritual destinies is in better hands than thine; a golden chain of covenant love links it to the eternal throne! That chain can never snap asunder. He who holds it in His hand gives thee *this* as the pledge of thy safety,—"Because I live, ye shall live also." "Why art thou then cast down, O my soul? and why art thou disquieted within me? *hope thou in God!*" Thou wilt assuredly ride out these stormy surges, and reach the desired haven. But be faithful with thyself: see that there be nothing to hinder or impede thy growth in grace. Think how little may retard thy progress. One sin indulged—one temptation tampered with—one bosom traitor, may cost thee many a bitter hour and bitter tear, by separating between thee and thy God. Make it thy daily prayer, "Search me, O God, and know my heart; try me and know my thoughts: and see if there be any wicked way in me, and lead me in the way everlasting."

"REMEMBER *THIS* WORD UNTO THY SERVANT, UPON WHICH THOU HAST CAUSED ME TO HOPE."

10TH DAY.

"He is Faithful that Promised."

"I have the keys of hell and of death."—REV. i. 18.

Dying Grace.

AND from whom could dying grace come so welcome, as from Thee, O blessed Jesus? Not only is Thy name, "The Abolisher of Death;" but Thou didst thyself *die!* Thou hast sanctified the grave by Thine own presence, and divested it of all its terrors. My soul! art thou at times afraid of this, thy last enemy? If the rest of thy pilgrimage-way be peaceful and unclouded, rests there a dark and portentous shadow over the terminating portals? Fear not! When that dismal entrance is reached, He who has "the keys of the grave and of death" suspended at His golden girdle, will impart grace to bear thee through. It is the messenger of peace. Thy Saviour calls thee! The promptings of nature, when, at first, thou seest the darkening waves, may be that of the affrighted disciples, when they said, "It is a spirit, and cried out for fear!" But a gentle voice will be heard high above the storm, "It is I! Be not afraid!" Death, indeed, as the wages of sin, must, even by the believer, be regarded as an enemy. But, oh! blessed thought, it is thy *last* enemy—the cause of thy last tear. In a few brief moments after that tear is shed, thy God will be wiping every vestige of it away? "O Death! where is thy sting? O Grave! where is thy victory? Thanks be unto God, who giveth us the victory through our Lord Jesus Christ!" Welcome, vanquished foe!—Birthday of heaven! —"to die is gain!"

"REMEMBER *THIS* WORD UNTO THY SERVANT, UPON WHICH THOU HAST CAUSED ME TO HOPE!"

11TH DAY.

"He is Faithful that Promised."

"The Lord will give grace and glory."—PSALM lxxxiv. 11.

After Grace; Glory.

OH! happy day, when this toilsome warfare will all be ended, Jordan crossed, Canaan entered, the legion-enemies of the wilderness no longer dreaded; sorrow, sighing, death, and, worst of all, *sin*, no more either to be felt or feared! Here is the terminating link in the golden chain of the everlasting covenant. It began with *predestination;* it ends with *glorification.* It began with sovereign grace in a bypast eternity, and no link will be awanting till the ransomed spirit be presented faultless before the throne! Grace and glory! If the earnest be sweet, what must be the reality? If the wilderness table contain such rich provision, what must be the glories of the eternal banqueting house? Oh! my soul, make sure of thine interest in the one, as the blessed prelude to the other. "Having access by faith into this *grace*, thou canst rejoice in hope of the *glory* of God;" for "whom He *justifies*, them He also *glorifies!*" Has grace begun in thee? Canst thou mark—though it should be but the drops of the incipient rill which is to terminate in such an ocean—the tiny grains which are to accumulate and issue in such "an exceeding weight of glory!" Delay not the momentous question! The day of offered grace is on the wing; its hours are fast numbering; and, "No grace, no glory!"

"REMEMBER *THIS* WORD UNTO THY SERVANT, UPON WHICH THOU HAST CAUSED ME TO HOPE!"

12TH DAY.

"He is Faithful that Promised."

"I will pray the Father, and He shall give you another Comforter, that He may abide with you for ever."—JOHN xiv. 16.

Another Comforter.

BLESSED Spirit of all grace! how oft have I grieved Thee! resisted Thy dealings, quenched Thy strivings; and yet art thou still pleading with me! Oh! let me realize more than I do the need of Thy gracious influences. Ordinances, sermons, communions, providential dispensations, are nothing without Thy life-giving power. "It is the Spirit that quickeneth." "No man can call Jesus, Lord, but by the Holy Ghost." Church of the living God! is not this one cause of thy deadness? My soul! is not this the secret of thy languishing frames, repeated declensions, uneven walk, and sudden falls, that the influences of the Holy Ghost are undervalued and unsought? Pray for the outpouring of this blessed Agent for the world's renovation, and thine own. "I will pour out my Spirit on all flesh," is the precursor of millennial bliss. Jesus! draw near, in thy mercy, to this torpid heart, as thou didst of old to thy mourning disciples, and breathe upon it, and say, "Receive ye the Holy Ghost." It is the mightiest of all boons; but, like the sun in the heavens, it is the freest of all: "For if ye, being evil, know how to give good gifts unto your children, how much more shall your Father in heaven give the Holy Spirit unto them that ask Him!"

"REMEMBER *THIS* WORD UNTO THY SERVANT, UPON WHICH THOU HAST CAUSED ME TO HOPE!"

13TH DAY.

"He is Faithful that Promised."

"All things work together for good to them that love God, to them who are the called according to His purpose." —ROM. viii. 28.

Providential Overruling. MY soul! be still! thou art in the hands of thy Covenant God. Were these strange vicissitudes in thy history the result of accident, or chance, thou mightest well be overwhelmed; but "*all things*," and *this* thing (be what it may) which may be now disquieting thee, is *one* of these "*all things*" that are *so* working mysteriously for thy good. Trust thy God! He will not deceive thee,—thy interests are with Him in safe custody. When sight says, "All these things are against me," let faith rebuke the hasty conclusion, and say, "Shall not the Judge of all the earth do right?" How often does God hedge up our way with thorns, to elicit simple trust! How seldom can we *see* all things so working for our good! But it is better discipline to *believe* it. Oh! for faith amid frowning providences, to say, "I *know* that thy judgments are good;" and, relying in the dark, to exclaim, "Though He slay me, yet will I trust Him!" Blessed Jesus! to thee are committed the reins of this universal empire. The same hand that was once nailed to the cross, is now wielding the sceptre on the throne,—"all power given unto thee in heaven and in earth." How can I doubt the wisdom, and faithfulness, and love, of the most mysterious earthly dealing, when I know that the Roll of Providence is thus in the hands of Him who has given the mightiest pledge Omnipotence *could* give of His tender interest in my soul's well-being, by giving *Himself* for me?

"REMEMBER *THIS* WORD UNTO THY SERVANT, UPON WHICH THOU HAST CAUSED ME TO HOPE!"

14TH DAY.

"He is Faithful that Promised."

"All the paths of the Lord are mercy and truth, unto such as keep His covenant and His testimonies."—PSALM xxv. 10.

Safe Walking.

THE paths of the Lord? My soul! never follow thine own paths. If thou dost so, thou wilt be in danger often of following sight rather than faith,—choosing the evil, and refusing the good. But "commit thy way unto the Lord, and He shall bring it to pass." Let this be thy prayer, "Show me *Thy* ways, O Lord; teach me *Thy* paths." Oh! for Caleb's spirit, "*wholly* to follow the Lord my God,"—to follow Him when self must be sacrificed, and hardship must be borne, and trials await me. To "walk with God,"—to ask in simple faith, "What wouldst thou have me to do?"—to have no will of my own, save this, that God's will is to be *my* will. Here is safety,—here is happiness. Fearlessly follow the Guiding Pillar. He will lead you by a *right* way, though it may be by a way of hardship, and crosses, and losses, and privations, to the city of habitation. Oh! the blessedness of thus lying passive in the hands of God; saying, "Undertake thou for me!"—dwelling with holy gratitude on past mercies and interpositions—taking these as pledges of future faithfulness and love—hearing His voice behind us, amid life's manifold perplexities, exclaiming, "This is the way, walk ye in it!" "Happy," surely, "are every people who are in such a case!" Happy, Reader! will it be for thee, if thou canst form the resolve in a strength greater than thine own: "This God shall be *my* God for ever and ever; He shall be my *Guide* even unto death!"

"REMEMBER *THIS* WORD UNTO THY SERVANT, UPON WHICH THOU HAST CAUSED ME TO HOPE!"

15TH DAY.

"He is Faithful that Promised."

"As many as I love, I rebuke and chasten."—REV. iii. 19.

Love in Chastisement.

SORROWING Believer! what couldst thou wish more than this? Thy furnace is severe; but look at this assurance of Him who lighted it. Love is the fuel that feeds its flames! Its every spark is love! Kindled by a Father's hand, and designed as a special pledge of a Father's love. How many of His dear children has He so rebuked and chastened; and all, *all* for one reason, "*I love them!*" The myriads in glory have passed through these furnace-fires,—*there* they were chosen,—*there* they were purified, sanctified, and made "vessels meet for the Master's use;" the dross and the alloy purged, that the pure metal might remain. And art thou to claim exemption from the same discipline? Art thou to think it strange concerning these same fiery trials that may be trying thee? Rather exult in them as thine adoption-privilege. Envy not those who are strangers to the refining flames,—who are "*without chastisement;*" rather, surely, the severest discipline *with* a *Father's love*, than the fullest earthly cup without that Father's smile. Oh! for grace to say, when the furnace is hottest, and the rod sorest, "Even so, *Father!*" And what, after all, is the severest of thy chastisements in comparison with what thy sins have deserved? Dost thou murmur under a Father's correcting love? What would it have been to have stood the wrath of an unpropitiated Judge, and that, too, *for ever?* Surely, in the light of eternity, the heaviest pang of earth is indeed "a light affliction!"

"REMEMBER *THIS* WORD UNTO THY SERVANT, UPON WHICH THOU HAST CAUSED ME TO HOPE!"

16TH DAY.

"He is Faithful that Promised."

"If need be."—1 PETER 1. 6.

A Condition in Chastisement.

THREE gracious words! Not one of all my tears shed for nought! Not one stroke of the rod unheeded, or that might have been spared? Thy heavenly Father loves thee too much, and too tenderly, to bestow harsher correction than thy case requires? Is it loss of health, or loss of wealth, or loss of beloved friends? Be still! there was a *need be.* We are no judges of what that "need be" is; often through aching hearts we are forced to exclaim, "Thy judgments are a great deep!" But God here pledges himself, that there will not be one redundant thorn in the believer's chaplet of suffering. No burden too heavy will be laid on him; and no sacrifice too great exacted *from* him. He will "temper the wind to the shorn lamb." Whenever the "need be" has accomplished its end, then the rod is removed—the chastisement suspended—the furnace quenched. "If need be!" Oh! what a pillow on which to rest thy aching head,—that there is not a drop in all thy bitter cup but what a God of love saw to be *absolutely* necessary! Wilt thou not trust Him, even though thou canst not trace the mystery of His dealings? Not too curiously prying into the "*Why* it is?" or "*How* it is?" but satisfied that "*So* it is," and, therefore that all *must* be well! "Although thou sayest, thou canst not see Him, yet judgment is before Him, *therefore* trust thou in Him!"

"REMEMBER *THIS* WORD UNTO THY SERVANT, UPON WHICH THOU HAST CAUSED ME TO HOPE!"

17TH DAY

"He is Faithful that Promised."

"A bruised reed shall He not break, and smoking flax shall He not quench."—MATT. xii. 20.

Strength in the Weak.

WILL Jesus accept such a heart as mine?—this erring, treacherous, traitor heart? The past! how many forgotten vows—broken covenants—prayerless days! How often have I made new resolutions, and as often has the reed succumbed to the first blast of temptation, and the burning flax been well-nigh quenched by guilty omissions and guiltier commissions! Oh! my soul! thou art low indeed,—the things that remain seem "ready to die." But thy Saviour-God will not give thee "over unto death." The reed is bruised; but He will not pluck it up by the roots. The flax is reduced to a smoking ember; but He will fan the decaying flame. Why wound thy loving Saviour's heart by these repeated declensions? He will not—*cannot* give thee up. Go, mourn thy weakness and unbelief. Cry unto the Strong for strength. Weary and faint one! thou hast an Omnipotent arm to lean on. "*He* fainteth not, neither is weary!" Listen to His own gracious assurance: "Fear not, for I am with thee. Be not dismayed, for I am thy God. I will *strengthen* thee; yea, I will help thee with the right hand of my righteousness!" Leaving all thy false props and refuges, be this thy resolve: "In the Lord put I my trust: why say ye to my soul, Flee as a bird to your mountain?"

REMEMBER *THIS* WORD UNTO THY SERVANT, UPON WHICH THOU HAST CAUSED ME TO HOPE."

18TH DAY.

"He is Faithful that Promised."

"Him that cometh unto me, I will in no wise cast out."—John vi. 37.

Encouragement to the Desponding.

"CAST out!" My soul! how oft might this have been thy history! Thou hast cast off thy God,—might He not oft have "cast out" thee? Yes! cast thee out as fuel for the fire of His wrath,—a sapless, fruitless cumberer. And yet, notwithstanding all thine ungrateful requital for His unmerited forbearance, He is still declaring, "As I live, saith the Lord, I have no pleasure in the death of him that dieth." Thy sins may be legion-like,—the sand of the sea may be their befitting type,—the thought of their turpitude and aggravation may be ready to overwhelm thee; but be still! thy patient God waits to be gracious! Oh! be deeply humbled and softened because of thy guilt, resolve to dedicate thyself anew to His service, and so coming, "He will *by no means* cast thee out!" Despond not by reason of former shortcomings,—thy sins are great, but thy Saviour's merits are greater. He is willing to forget all the past, and sink it in oblivion, if there be present love, and the promise of future obedience. "Simon, son of Jonas, *lovest thou me?*" Ah! how different is God's verdict from man's! After such sins as thine, man's sentence would have been, "*I* will in nowise receive!" But "it is better to fall into the hands of God, than into the hands of man;" for He says, "I will in *nowise* cast out!"

"REMEMBER *THIS* WORD UNTO THY SERVANT, UPON WHICH THOU HAST CAUSED ME TO HOPE!"

19TH DAY.

"He is Faithful that Promised."

"Peace I leave with you; my peace I give unto you; not as the world giveth."—JOHN xiv. 27.

Peace in Believing. "THOU wilt keep him in perfect peace whose mind is stayed on Thee." "Perfect peace!"—what a blessed attainment! My soul! is it thine? Sure I am it is *not*, if thou art seeking it in a perishable world, or in the perishable creature, or in thy perishable self. Although thou hast all that the world would call enviable and happy, unless thou hast peace *in* God, and *with* God, all else is unworthy of the name;—a spurious thing, which the first breath of adversity will shatter, and the hour of death utterly annihilate! Perfect peace! What is it? It is the peace of forgiveness. It is the peace arising out of a sense of God reconciled through the blood of the everlasting covenant,

—resting sweetly on the bosom, and the work of Jesus,—to Him committing thine eternal all. My soul! stay thyself on God, that so this blessed peace may be thine. Thou hast tried the world. It has deceived thee. Prop after prop of earthly scaffolding has yielded, and tottered, and fallen. Has thy God ever done so? Ah! this false and counterfeit world-peace may do well for the world's work, and the world's day of prosperity. But test it in the hour of sorrow; and what can it do for thee when most it is needed? On the other hand, what though thou hast no other blessing on earth to call thine own? Thou art rich indeed, if thou canst look upwards to Heaven, and say with "unpresumptuous smile," "I am at peace with God."

REMEMBER *THIS* WORD UNTO THY SERVANT, UPON WHICH THOU HAST CAUSED ME TO HOPE!"

20TH DAY.

"He is Faithful that Promised."

"Blessed are the dead that die in the Lord."—REV. xiv. 13.

Bliss in Dying.

MY Soul! is this blessedness thine in prospect? Art thou ready, if called this night to lie down on thy death-pillow, sweetly to fall asleep in Jesus? What is the sting of death? It is sin. Is death, then, to thee, robbed of its sting, by having listened to the gracious accents of pardoning love, "Be of good cheer, thy sins, which are many, are all forgiven thee?" If thou hast made up thy peace with God, resting on the work and atoning blood of His dear Son, then is the Last Enemy divested of all his terror, and thou canst say, in sweet composure, of thy dying couch and dying hour,—"I will both lay me down in peace and sleep, because Thou, Lord, makest me to dwell in safety!" Reader! ponder that solemn question,

"Am I ready to die? Am I living as I should wish I had done when that last hour arrives?" And when shall it arrive? To-morrow is not thine. "Verily, there may be but a step between thee and death." Oh! solve the question speedily,—risk no doubts and no peradventure. Every day is proclaiming anew the lesson, "The race is not to the swift, nor the battle to the strong." Seek to live, so that that hour cannot come upon thee too soon, or too unexpectedly. Live a dying life! How blessed to live,—how blessed to die, with the consciousness, that there may be but a step between thee and glory!

"REMEMBER *THIS* WORD UNTO THY SERVANT, UPON WHICH THOU HAST CAUSED ME TO HOPE!"

21st Day.

"He is Faithful that Promised."

"In due season we shall reap, if we faint not."—Gal. vi. 9.

A Due Reaping. Believer! all the glory of thy salvation belongs to Jesus,—none to thyself; every jewel in thine eternal crown is His,—purchased by His blood, and polished by His Spirit. The confession of time will be the ascription of all eternity: "By the grace of God I am what I am!" But though "all be of grace," thy God calls thee to personal strenuousness in the work of thy high calling;—to "labour," to "fight," to "wrestle," to "*agonize*;" and the heavenly reaping will be in proportion to the earthly sowing: "He that soweth sparingly, shall reap also sparingly; and he that soweth bountifully, shall reap also bountifully!" What an incentive to holy living, and increased spiritual attainments! My soul! wouldst thou be a star shining high and bright in the firmament of glory?—wouldst thou receive the ten-talent recompense? Then be not weary. Gird on thine armour for fresh conquests. Be gaining daily some new victory over sin. Deny thyself. Be a willing cross-bearer for thy Lord's sake. Do good to all men as thou hast opportunity; be patient under provocation, "slow to wrath," resigned in trial. Let the world take knowledge of thee that thou art wearing Christ's livery, and bearing Christ's spirit, and sharing Christ's cross. And when the reaping time comes, He who has promised that the cup of cold water cannot go unrecompensed, will not suffer thee to lose thy reward!

"REMEMBER *THIS* WORD UNTO THY SERVANT, UPON WHICH THOU HAST CAUSED ME TO HOPE!"

22D DAY.

"He is Faithful that Promised."

"The days of thy mourning shall be ended."—ISAIAH lx. 20.

An End of Weeping.

CHRIST'S people are a weeping band, though there be much in this lovely world to make them joyous and happy. Yet when they think of sin—their own sin, and the unblushing sins of a world in which their God is dishonoured—need we wonder at their tears?—that they should be called "Mourners," and their pilgrimage-home a "Valley of Tears?" Bereavement, and sickness, and poverty, and death, following the track of sin, add to their mourning experience; and with many of God's best beloved, one tear is scarce dried when another is ready to flow! Mourners! rejoice! When the reaping time comes, the weeping time ends! When the white robe and the golden harp are bestowed, every remnant of the sackcloth attire is removed. The moment the pilgrim, whose forehead is here furrowed with woe, bathes it in the crystal river of life,—that moment the pangs of a life-time of sorrow are eternally forgotten! Reader! if thou art one of these care-worn ones, the days of thy mourning are numbered! A few more throbbings of this aching heart, and then the angel who proclaims "time," shall proclaim also, sorrow, and sighing, and mourning, to "be no longer!" Seek now to mourn thy sins more than thy sorrows; reserve thy bitterest tears for forgetfulness of thy dear Lord. The saddest and sorest of all bereavements, is when the sins which have separated thee from Him, evoke the anguish-cry, "Where is my God?"

"REMEMBER *THIS* WORD UNTO THY SERVANT, UPON WHICH THOU HAST CAUSED ME TO HOPE!"

23D DAY.

"He is Faithful that Promised."

"Behold, I come quickly."—REV. iii. 11.

A Speedy Coming. "EVEN so! come, Lord Jesus!" "Why tarry the wheels of Thy chariot?" Six thousand years this world has rolled on, getting hoary with age, and wrinkled with sins and sorrows. A waiting Church sees the long-drawn shadows of twilight announcing, "The Lord is at hand." Prepare, my soul, to meet Him. Oh! happy days, when thine adorable Redeemer, so long dishonoured and despised, shall be publicly enthroned, in presence of an assembled universe, crowned Lord of All, glorified in His saints, satisfied in the fruits of His soul's travail, destroying His enemies with the brightness of His coming—the lightning-glance of wrath,—causing the hearts of His exulting people to "rejoice with joy unspeakable and full of glory." Prepare, my soul, to meet Him! Let it be a joyous thought to thee,—thy "blessed hope,"—the meeting of thine Elder Brother. Stand oftentimes on the watchtower to catch the first streak of that coming brightness, the first murmur of these chariot wheels. The world is now in preparation! It is rocking on its worn-out axle. There are voices on every side proclaiming, "He cometh! He cometh! to judge the earth." Reader! art thou among the number of those who "love His appearing?" Remember the attitude of His expectant saints: "Blessed are those servants whom the Lord, when He cometh, will find WATCHING!"

"REMEMBER *THIS* WORD UNTO THY SERVANT, UPON WHICH THOU HAST CAUSED ME TO HOPE!"

24TH DAY.

"He is Faithful that Promised."

"At evening-time it shall be light."—ZECH. xiv. 7.

Eventide Light. How inspiring the thought of coming glory! How would we rise above our sins, and sorrows, and sufferings, if we could live under the power of "a world to come!" Were faith to take at all times its giant leap beyond a soul-trammelling earth, and remember its brighter destiny. If it could stand on its Pisgah Mount, and look above and beyond the mists and vapours of this land of shadows, and rest on the "better country." But, alas! in spite of ourselves, the wings ofttimes refuse to soar—the spirit droops—guilty fears depress—sin dims and darkens—God's providences seem to frown—God's ways are misinterpreted—the Christian belies his name and his destiny. But, "At eventide it shall be light."—The material sun, which wades through clouds and a troubled sky, sets often in a couch of lustrous gold? So, when the sun of life is setting, many a ray of light will shoot athwart memory's darkened sky, and many mysterious dealings of the wilderness will then elicit an "All is well!" How frequently is the presence and upholding grace of Jesus especially felt and acknowledged at that hour, and griefs and misgivings hushed with His own gentle accents, "Fear not! it is I; be not afraid." A triumphant death-bed! It is no unmeaning word; the eye is lighted with holy lustre, the tongue with holy rapture, as if the harps of heaven were stealing on it. My soul! may such a life's evening-tide be thine!

"REMEMBER *THIS* WORD UNTO THY SERVANT, UPON WHICH THOU HAST CAUSED ME TO HOPE!"

25TH DAY.

"He is Faithful that Promised."

"What I do thou knowest not now; but thou shalt know hereafter."—JOHN xiii. 7.

Heavenly Illumination. As the natural sun sometimes sinks in clouds, so, occasionally, the Christian who has a bright rising, and a brighter meridian, sets in gloom. It is not *always* "light" at his evening-time; but this we know, that when the day of immortality breaks, the last vestige of earth's shadows will for ever flee away. To the closing hour of time, Providence may be to him a baffling enigma: but ere the first hour has struck on heaven's chronometer, all will be clear. My soul! "in God's light thou shalt see light;" the Book of His decrees is a sealed book now,—"A great deep" is all the explanation thou canst often give to His judgments; the *why* and the *wherefore* He seems to keep from us, to test our faith, to discipline us in trustful submission, and lead us to say, "Thy will be done!" But rejoice in that hereafter-light which awaits thee! Now we see through a glass darkly; but *then*, face to face. In the great mirror of eternity all the events of this chequered scene will be reflected; the darkest of them will be seen to be bright with mercy,—the severest dispensations, "only the severer aspects of His love!" Pry not, then, too curiously; pronounce not too censoriously on God's dealings with thee. Wait with patience till the grand day of disclosures; one confession shall then burst from every tongue, "Righteous art thou, O Lord!"

"REMEMBER *THIS* WORD UNTO THY SERVANT, UPON WHICH THOU HAST CAUSED ME TO HOPE."

26TH DAY.

"He is Faithful that Promised."

"I will come again, and receive you unto myself, that where I am, there ye may be also."—JOHN xiv. 3.

A Glorious Reunion.

IF the meeting of a long absent friend, or brother, on earth, be a joyous event, what, my soul, must be the joy of thy union with this Brother of brothers, this Friend of friends! "I will come again!" Oh! what an errand of love, what a promised honour and dignity is this!—His saints to share, not His Heaven only, but His immediate presence. "Where *I am*, *there ye* shall be also!" "Father, I *will* (it was His dying wish,—a wondrous codicil in that testamentary prayer) that those whom Thou hast given me be with me where *I am*." Happy reunion! Blessed Saviour, if Thy presence be so sweet on a sin-stricken earth, and when known only by the invisible eye of faith, what must be that presence in a sinless Heaven, unfolded in all its unutterable loveliness and glory! Happy reunion! it will be a meeting of the whole ransomed family—the Head with all its members—the Vine with all its branches—the Shepherd with all His flock—the Elder Brother with all His kinsmen. Oh, the joy, too, of mutual recognition among the death-divided—ties snapt asunder on earth, indissolubly renewed—severed friendships reunited—the triumph of love complete—love binding brother with brother, and friend with friend, and *all* to the Elder Brother! My soul! what thinkest thou of this Heaven? Remember who it is that Jesus says shall sit with Him upon His throne,—"Him that overcometh."

"REMEMBER *THIS* WORD UNTO THY SERVANT, UPON WHICH THOU HAST CAUSED ME TO HOPE!"

27TH DAY.

"He is Faithful that Promised."

"And I will betroth thee unto Me for ever."—HOSEA ii. 19.

Everlasting Espousals. How wondrous and varied are the figures which Jesus employs to express the tenderness of His covenant love! My soul! thy Saviour-God hath "married thee!" Wouldst thou know the hour of thy betrothment? Go back into the depths of a by-past eternity, before the world was; then and there, thine espousals were contracted: "I have loved thee with an everlasting love." Soon shall the bridal-hour arrive, when thine absent Lord shall come to welcome His betrothed bride into His royal palace. "The Bridegroom tarrieth;" but see that thou dost not slumber and sleep! Surely there is much all around demanding the girded loins and the burning lamps. At "midnight!" (the hour when He is least expected) the cry *may* be—*shall* be heard,—"Behold, the Bridegroom cometh!" My soul! has this mystic union been formed between thee and thy Lord? Canst thou say, in humble assurance of thine affiance in Him, "My beloved is mine, and I am His!" If so, great, unspeakably great, are the glories which await thee! Thy dowry, as the bride of Christ, is all that Omnipotence can bestow, and all that a feeble creature can receive. In the prospect of those glorious nuptials, thou needest dread no pang of widowhood. What God has joined together, no created power can take asunder; He betroths thee, and it is—"for ever!"

"REMEMBER *THIS* WORD UNTO THY SERVANT, UPON WHICH THOU HAST CAUSED ME TO HOPE!"

28TH DAY.

"He is Faithful that Promised."

"This corruptible must put on incorruption."—1 COR. xv. 53.

A Joyful Resurrection.

MARVEL of marvels? The sleeping ashes of the sepulchre starting at the tones of the archangel's trumpet!—the dishonoured dust rising a glorified body, like its risen Lord's? At death, the soul's bliss is perfect in kind; but this bliss is not complete in degree, until reunited to the tabernacle it has left behind to mingle with the sods of the valley. But tread lightly on that grave, it contains precious, because ransomed dust! My body, as well as my spirit, was included in the redemption price of Calvary; and "them also which sleep in Jesus will God bring with Him." Oh! blessed Jubilee-day of creation, when Christ's "dead men shall arise;"—when, together with His dead body, they shall come; and the summons shall sound forth, "Awake, and sing, ye that dwell in the dust!" All the joys of that resurrection morn we cannot tell; but its chief glory we *do* know,—"When He shall appear, we shall be like Him; for we shall see Him as He is." Like Him!—My soul, art thou waiting this manifestation of the sons of God? Like Him!—Hast thou caught up any faint resemblance to that all-glorious image? Having this hope in thee, art thou purifying thyself, even as He is pure? Be much with Jesus now, that thou mayst exult in meeting Him hereafter. Thus taking Him as thy Guide and Portion in life, thou mayst lay thee down in thy dark and noisome cell, and look forward with triumphant hope to the dawn of a resurrection morn, saying, "What time I awake, I am still with Thee!"

"REMEMBER *THIS* WORD UNTO THY SERVANT, UPON WHICH THOU HAST CAUSED ME TO HOPE!"

29TH DAY.

"He is Faithful that Promised."

"There shall be no night there."—REV. xxi. 25.

A Nightless Heaven.

MY soul! is it night with thee here? Art thou wearied with these midnight tossings on life's tumultuous sea? Be still! the day is breaking! soon shall thy Lord appear. "His going forth is prepared as the morning." That glorious appearing shall disperse every cloud, and usher in an eternal noontide which knows no twilight. "Thy sun shall no more go down, neither shall thy moon withdraw itself; for the Lord shall be thine everlasting light." Everlasting light! Wondrous secret of a nightless world!—the glories of a present God!—the everlasting light of the Three in One, quenching the radiance of all created orbs—superseding all material luminaries. "My soul waiteth for the Lord more than they that watch for the morning!" The haven is nearing—star after star is quenched in more glorious effulgence—every bound over these dark waves is bringing thee nearer the eternal shore. Wilt thou not, then, humbly and patiently endure "weeping for the night," in the prospect of the "joy that cometh in the morning?" Strange realities! a world without night—a firmament without a sun; and, greater wonder still, *thyself* in this world,—a joyful denizen of this nightless, sinless, sorrowless, tearless Heaven!—basking underneath the Fountain of uncreated light! No exhaustion of glorified body and spirit to require repose; no lassitude or weariness to suspend the ever-deepening song:—"They *rest not!*"

"REMEMBER *THIS* WORD UNTO THY SERVANT, UPON WHICH THOU HAST CAUSED ME TO HOPE."

30TH DAY.

"He is Faithful that Promised."

"When the Chief Shepherd shall appear, ye shall receive a crown of glory that fadeth not away."—1 PETER v. 4.

A Crown of Life.

WHAT! is the beggar to be "raised from the dunghill, set among princes, and made to inherit a throne of glory?" is dust and ashes, a puny rebel, a guilty traitor, to be pitied, pardoned, loved, exalted from the depths of despair, raised to the heights of Heaven—gifted with kingly honour—royally fed—royally clothed—royally attended—and, at last, royally crowned? O my soul, look forward with joyous emotion to that day of wonders, when He whose head shall be crowned with many crowns, shall be the dispenser of royal diadems to His people; and when they shall begin the joyful ascription of all eternity, "Unto Him that loved us and washed us from our sins in His own blood, and has made us

KINGS——; to Him be glory and dominion for ever and ever. Amen." Wilt thou not be among the number? Shall the princes and monarchs of the earth wade through seas of blood for a corruptible crown; and wilt thou permit thyself to lose the incorruptible, or barter it for some perishable nothings of earth? Oh! that thou wouldst awake to thy high destiny, and live up to thy transcendant privileges as the citizen of a Kingly Commonwealth, a member of the blood-royal of Heaven. What wouldst thou not sacrifice,—what effort wouldst thou grudge, if thou wert included at last in the gracious benediction, "Come, ye blessed of My Father, inherit the kingdom prepared for you from the foundation of the world?"

"REMEMBER *THIS* WORD UNTO THY SERVANT, UPON WHICH THOU HAST CAUSED ME TO HOPE!"

31st Day.

"He is Faithful that Promised."

"God himself shall be with them, and be their God. And God shall wipe away all tears from their eyes; and there shall be no more death, neither sorrow, nor crying, neither shall there be any more pain: for the former things are passed away."—Rev. xxi. 3, 4.

The Vision and Fruition of God.

Glorious consummation! All the other glories of Heaven are but emanations from this glory that excelleth. Here is the focus and centre to which every ray of light converges. God is "all in all." Heaven *without God!*—it would send a thrill of dismay through the burning ranks of angels and archangels; it would dim every eye, and hush every harp, and change the whitest robe into sackcloth. And shall I then, indeed, *see God?*" What! shall I gaze on these inscrutable glories, and live? Yes, God himself shall be with them, and be their God: they shall "*see his face!*" And not only the vision, but the *fruition*. Oh! how does sin in my holiest moments damp the enjoyment of Him! It is the "pure in heart" alone who can "see," far more, who can enjoy "God." Even if he did reveal himself *now*, these eyes could never endure His intolerable brightness. But *then*, with a heart purified from corruption—a world where the taint of sin and the power of temptation never enters—the soul again a bright mirror, reflecting the lost image of the Godhead—all the affections devoted to their original high destiny—the love of God the motive principle, the ruling passion—the glory of God the undivided object and aim—the will no opposing or antagonist bias,—man will, for the first time, know all the blessedness of his chief end,—"to glorify God, and to enjoy Him for ever!"

"REMEMBER *THIS* WORD UNTO THY SERVANT, UPON WHICH THOU HAST CAUSED ME TO HOPE!"

All

The Promises of God

In Him

Are Yea and in Him

Amen.

Butler, Rev. C. M. Old Truths and New Errors. 16mo. 50 cts.
Canticles of the Church. $1 per dozen.
Carrie; or, the Child of the Parsonage. 18mo. 38 cts.
Castleman. Plain Sermons. 12mo. $1 00.
Cecil and his Dog. A Tale for the Young. 16mo. 75 cts.
Chapin. The Primitive Church. 12mo. 75 cts.
Chapin—Puritanism not Protestantism. 50 cts.
Child's Christian Year. By Miss Tuthill. 18mo. 38 cts.
Christian's Companion to the Sick and Afflicted. 8vo. 38 cts.
Christian Graces. 12mo. 75 cts.
Christian Year. By Rev. J. Keble. With Bp. Doane's Notes. 32mo. 50 cts.
Christian's Manual. By Bishop Hobart. 16mo. 75 cts.
Christ's Warning to the Churches. By Rev. J. Lathrop. 16mo. 38 cts.
Church Chant Book. By Rev. Wm. Staunton. 4to. 75 cts.
Church Choir. By Rev. J. Muenscher, D. D. 8vo. $1 00.
Church Register for Parish Records. From $6 00 to $12 50.
Churchman Armed. 12mo. $1 00.
Churchman's Heavenly Hours. 32mo. 31 cts.
Claxton's Questions on the Gospels. Parts I. & II. 12 cts. each.
Clergyman's Companion. By Bishop Hobart. 12mo.
Coleridge. Aids to Reflection. Edited by Dr. McVickar. 12mo. 75 cts.
Colton, Rev. C. Mission of the Prot. Epis. Church. $1 00.
Communicant's Companion. 25 cts.
Communicant's Manual. (The Altar.) 32mo. 25 cts.
Cousin Bertha's Stories. By Mrs. M'Donald. 18mo. 38 cts.
Cross of Christ. By Hook. 50 cts.
Cunningham's, Rev. J. W., Sermons. 8vo. $1 00.
Cunningham—Velvet Cushion. 18mo. Illustrated. 38 cts.
Dairyman's Daughter. By Rev. L. Richmond. 32mo. 19 cts.
Dehon on Confirmation. 18mo. 13 cts.
Devout Communicant. By Bickersteth. 32mo. 31 cts.
Devotion for Family and Closet. By a Country Clergyman. 12mo. 50 cts.
Deus Misereatur. From Zingarelli's celebrated Miserere. 25 cts.
Dew of Heaven. From Eminent Divines. 32mo. 31 cts.
Divine History of the Church. $1 00.
Doctrine of the Cross. Illustrated. 16mo. 50 cts.
Domestic and Religious Life in Italy. Edited by Bp. Kip. 16mo. 63 cts.
Dorr's Recognition of Friends. 32mo. 25 cts.
Double Witness of the Church. By Bishop Kip. $1 00.
Duffie's, Rev. C. R., Sermons. 2 vols. 8vo. $3 00.
Dyer, Rev. P., on Episcopacy. 12mo. 25 cts.

English Churchwomen of the XVIIth Century. 18mo. 63 cts.
Essays on Episcopacy. 8vo. 50 cts.
Eusebius, Ecclesiastical History of. $2 25.
Explanatory History of the Book of Common Prayer. 18mo. 38 cts.
Faber, Rev. G. S., on Romanism. 12mo. 75 cts.
Faber—On Doctrine of Election. 8vo. $1 75.
Faithful Promiser, with The Words of Jesus. 18mo. 38 cts.
Family and Closet Devotions. 12mo. 50 cts.
Festivals and Fasts. By Bp. J. H. Hobart. 12mo. 75 cts.
Fowler, Rev. A., on the Common Prayer. 12mo. 75 cts.
Fox's, Rev. G. T., Sermons. 8vo. $1 00.
Frank the Painter. Illustrated.
Fry's, Mrs. Elizabeth, Memoirs. By Timpson. 12mo. 75 cts.
Gibson's, Bp., Pastoral Letters, and Horne on Infidelity. 12mo. 75 cts.
Gregorian Chants. With Additions by Dr. Hodges. 25 cts.
Gregory the Seventh. By J. W. Bowden. $1 25.
Grace Church Music. Large folio. $2 00.
Greatorex's Church Music. $1 00.
Gregorian and other Ecclesiastical Chants. 25 cts.
Hale's, Rev. Dr., on the Morning and Evening Prayer. 18mo. 25 cts.
Hammond. Definitions of Faith. 12mo. $1 25.
Hanson's Reply to Bishop Ives. 12mo. 12 cts.
Happiness of the Blessed. By Bishop Mant. 12mo. 75 cts.
Happy Old Age. Exemplified in the Life of Mrs. Bolton. 32mo. 19 cts.
Hawkstone. A Tale of and for England. 12mo. $1 50.
Hay, Rev. A., on Baptism. 18mo. 25 cts.
Heber's Last Days. By Archdeacon Robinson. 12mo. 50 cts.
Hening, Mrs. African Mission of the Prot. Epis. Church. 12mo. 75 cts.
History of the Society for Propagating the Gospel. 75 cts.
Hobart—Posthumous Works. 3 vols. 8vo. $5 00.
Hobart—Revision of Claude on the Composition of a Sermon. 12mo. 63 cts.
Hobart—State of the Departed. 12mo. 50 cts.
Hodges. Infant Baptism tested by Scripture. 12mo. 50 cts.
Hoffman. Law of the Prot. Epis. Church in the U. S. 8vo. $2 00.
Holmes, Mrs. Scenes in our Parish. 12mo. $1 00.
Hopkins, Bp. Primitive Church compared. 12mo. $1 00.
Hopkins—Church of Rome. 12mo. $1 00.
Hopkins—Essays on Gothic Architecture, Plans and Drawings. 4to. $2 00.

Hopkins—Lectures on the Reformation. 12mo. 75 cts.
Horne's, Bp., Works. 2 vols. Royal 8vo. $4 50.
Horne on the Psalms, &c. $2 00.
Horne's Discourses. 8vo. $2 50.
Horne on Infidelity, and Gibson's Pastoral Letters. 75 cts.
Humphrey's Miscellaneous Works. 8vo. $1 50.
Hymns on the Church Catechism. 18mo. 31 cts.
Ives' Catechism. 18mo. Part I. 6 cts.
Ives' Catechism. 18mo. Part II. 6 cts.
Ives—Sermons on the Obedience of Faith. 16mo. 38 cts.
Jackson, Rev. Wm. Life and Sermons. 8vo. $1 25.
Jarvis, Rev. Dr. Discourses on the Prophecy. 50 cts.
Jebb, Rev. John, D. D. Piety without Asceticism. 75 cts.
Jenks. Offices of Devotion. 16mo. 63 cts.
Jerram and Wall. On Infant Baptism. 16mo. 63 cts.
Jewell, Bp. Apology for the Church of England. 12mo. 75 cts.
Jones, Rev. Wm. Doctrine of the Trinity. 16mo. 50 cts.
Keble. Lyra Innocentium. 12mo. 75 cts.
Kip's, Bp., Double Witness of the Church. 12mo. $1 00.
Kip—Early Conflicts of Christianity. 12mo. 75 cts.
Kip—Lenten Fast. 12mo. 63 cts.
Kip—Confession of a Convert to Romanism. 63 cts.
Law, Rev. W. Serious Call to a Holy Life. 12mo. 75 cts.
Lee, Bp. Life of the Apostle Peter. 16mo. 75 cts.
Lewis. Sermons for the Christian Year. 8vo. $1 25.
Lewis—Confession of Christ. 12mo. 38 cts.
Lewis—Position of the Prot. Epis. Church. 3 cts.
Little Elsie and Little Jemmy. (For Children.) 18mo. 25 cts.
Little Carrie; or, the Child of the Parsonage. 38 cts.
Lives of Hale, Rochester, &c. 12mo. 75 cts.
Manning's, Archdeacon, Sermons. 3 vols., 8vo. $3 75.
Mant and D'Oyly's Bible. Edited by Bp. Hobart. 3 vols.
Mant and D'Oyly's New Testament. $2 50.
Mant, Bp. Happiness of the Blessed. 12mo. 75 cts.
Mant—On Reading Church Liturgy. 12mo. 75 cts.
Manual of Confirmation and Communion. 18mo. 25 cts.
Mason. Selections from the Fathers. In Latin. 12mo. 75 cts.
McIlvaine's, Bp., Discourses. 2 vols. 8vo. $4 50.
McIlvaine—Reasons for Refusing to Consecrate a Church. 25 c.
Meade, Bp., on the Pastoral Office. 8vo. $1 25.
Melvill's Rev. H., Sermons. 2 vols. 8vo. $3 50.
Melvill—Lectures on Practical Subjects. 1 vol. $1 50.
Mercy to Babes. By Rev. Wm. Adams. 12mo. 62 cts.
Miller's, Rev. Dr., Retrospect of the XVIIIth Century. $2 50.
Moore's, Bp., Sermons. 2 vols. 8vo. $3 00.
More, Hannah. Spirit of Prayer. 32mo. 25 cts.

More—Private Devotions. 32mo. 25 cts.
Murdock. New Testament: Literal Translation. 8vo. $2 00.
Murdock—Ecclesiastical History. By Mosheim. 3 vols. $6 50.
Neander. History of the Church. 8vo. $1 75.
Nelson's Greek Exercises. Edited by Prof. Anthon. 50 cts.
Newnham's Tribute of Sympathy. 12mo. 50 cts.
Odenheimer—Devout Churchman's Companion. 63 cts.
Odenheimer—Origin of the Prayer Book. 32mo. 25 cts.
Odenheimer—True Catholic no Romanist. 32mo. 25 cts.
Odenheimer—Young Churchman Catechized. 16 cts.
Oral Catechism. On the Principles of Religion. Part I., 6 cts.
Oral Catechism. On the Bible. Part II., 6 cts.
Paget's Rev. F. E., Sermons on Daily Life. 12mo. 1 00.
Palmer. Ecclesiastical History. 12mo. 50 cts.
Plain Sermons. By Authors of "Tracts for the Times." $1 50.
Questions on Self-Examination. 32mo. 10 cts.
Religion as Seen through the Church. 16mo. 50 cts.
Richardson, Rev. N. S. On Confirmation. 32mo. 8 cts.
Richardson—Reasons why I am not a Papist. 12mo. 12 cts.
Secker, Archbp. On Church Catechism. 12mo. 75 cts.
Secker—Lectures on Popery. 18mo. 25 cts.
Selectæ e Patribus, seu Theologica Summa Clericis Haud Inutile in Usum Juventutis Academicæ. 12mo. 75 cts.
Scenes in Our Parish. 12mo. $1 00.
Short, Bp. Church of England. 8vo. $1 50.
Short—What is Christianity? 50 cts.
Skinner's, Bp., Truth and Order. 8vo. $1 00.
Smith's, Rev. Wm., Primitive Psalmody. 12mo. 50 cts.
Smith, J. A. Moral and Physical Science. $1 50.
Spencer. History of the Reformation in England. 16mo. 50 cts.
Spincke's Manual of Devotion. 16mo. 75 cts.
Stanford, Rev. Dr. John. Memoir and Life. 12mo. 75 cts.
Stanley on the Parables. For Sunday Schools. 18mo. 38 cts.
Staunton. A Dictionary of the Church. $1 25.
Steps to the Altar. 25 cts.
Stone, Rev. Dr. Church Universal. 8vo. $1 25.
Stone—Address on the Death of Dr. Milnor. 25 cts.
Sumner's Exposition. Cloth, 75 cts.
Sunday School Teacher's Companion. 18mo. 38 cts.
Sunlight through the Mist. 75 cts.
Tayler, Rev. C. B. Mark Wilton. 12mo. 75 cts.
Tayler—Angels' Song. 12mo. 75 cts.
Tayler—Legends and Records. 75 cts.
Tayler—Earnestness. 75 cts.
Tayler—Lady Mary. 12mo. 75 cts.
Tayler—Margaret; or, The Pearl. 12mo. 75 cts.

Tayler—Records of a Good Man's Life. 12mo. 75 cts.
Tayler—Scenes in a Clergyman's Life. 12mo. 75 cts.
Tayler—Thankfulness. 12mo. 75 cts.
Tayler—Truth; or, Persis Clareton. 12mo. 75 cts.
Tayler—Arthur and his Mother. 18mo. 38 cts.
The Pointed Psalter for Chanting. 18mo. 38 cts.
The People's Psalter. By Dr. Muhlenberg. 38 cts.
The Vast Army. By the Rev. Edward Monro. 18mo. 38 cts.
The Manuscript Chant Book. By George F. Jones. $1 50.
Thomas à Kempis. Imitation of Christ. 16mo. 75 cts.
Thornton. Family Prayers. 12mo. 75 cts.
Totten's, Rev. S., Analogy of Truth. 12mo. 50 cts.
Trimmer, Mrs., on the Church Catechism. 18mo. 25 cts.
Trimmer—Easy Lessons. 24mo. 13 cts.
Trimmer—Scripture History. 18mo. 25 cts.
Turner, Rev. Dr., New Testament by Parallel References. 12mo. 25 cts.
Turner—A Companion to the Book of Genesis. 8vo. $1 25.
Turner—Epistle to the Romans, Greek and English. $1 50.
Turner—Epistle to the Hebrews, Greek and English. $1 25.
Turner—Distinguished Jewish Rabbies. 12mo. 75 cts.
Turner—Scripture Prophecy. 75 cts.
Two Sisters; or, Principle and Practice. 75 cts.
Tyng, Rev. S. H., on Confirmation. 32mo. 25 cts.
Tyng—Address on the Death of Dr. Milnor. 8vo. 25 cts.
Wainwright, Bp. Order of Family Prayer. 12mo. 75 cts.
Wainwright—Short Family Prayers. 25 cts.
Wainwright—Sermons on Religious Education. 8vo. 50 cts.
Wainwright and Muhlenberg. Choir and Family Psalter. 4to. $2 00.
Wainwright—Music of the Church. Enlarged. $1 00.
Wall on Baptism. 16mo. 63 cts.
White Bp. On the Ordination Office. 12mo. 75 cts.
Whole Duty of Man. 12mo. 75 cts.
Who is Jesus? 18mo. Cloth. 25 cts.
Wilberforce, Bp. Family Prayers. 18mo. 25 cts.
Wilberforce, Bp. Protestant Episcopal Church in America. 12mo. $1 00.
Williams, Bp., on the Gospel Miracles. 16mo. 38 cts.
Williams, Rev. Isaac, on the Lord's Passion. Cloth, 75 cts.
Words of Jesus and Faithful Promiser. 38 cts.
Wilson, Bp., on Confirmation. 32mo. 25 cts.
Wilson—On the True Understanding of the Lord's Supper. 32mo. 38 cts.
Wilson—Sacra Privata. 18mo. 38 cts. 16mo. 75 cts.
Wilson—Sacra Privata, and Bp. Andrewes' Devotions. 75 cts.

CHURCH MUSIC.

The Music of the Church. A Collection of Psalm, Hymn, and Chant Tunes, adapted to the worship of the Protestant Episcopal Church in the United States. New edition, much improved, By Wainwright. $1 00.

The Church Choir. A Collection of Sacred Music, comprising a great variety of Psalm and Hymn Tunes, Anthems and Chants. Arranged for the Organ and Piano Forte. By Rev. Joseph Muenscher, D. D. $1 25.

New York Grace Church Collection of Sacred Music. Selected and arranged from the Classical and Sacred Works of the Great Composers, and adapted to the Psalms and Hymns of the Protestant Episcopal Church. With separate Organ Accompaniment. By William A. King, Organist and Director of the Music of Grace Church, New York. $2 00.

The Church Chant Book. Comprising a large and varied selection of Chant Tunes, in the Gregorian and Modern Modes, adapted to the Ordinary and Extraordinary Services of the Protestant Episcopal Church; with an Introduction and Instructions relative to the Mode of Performance. Written, Arranged, and in part Composed, by the Rev. William Staunton. 75 cts.

The Choir and Family Psalter. Being the Psalms of David, together with the Canticles of the Morning and Evening Prayer, and Occasional Offices of the Church, arranged for Chanting. To which is prefixed a Selection of Chants. By Wainwright and Muhlenberg. $2 00.

Greatorex's Church Music. Being a Collection of Psalm and Hymn Tunes, Chants, Anthems, and Sentences, Original and Selected, from the best Standard Composers, adapted for the use of the Protestant Episcopal Church in America, and for Congregations of other Denominations, as well as for Societies and Schools. By H. W. Greatorex, Organist and Director of the Music in Calvary Church, New York. $1 00.

The People's Psalter. Being the Psalms of David, arranged for Chanting. With an Appendix containing Hymns from Holy Scripture, and a Selection of Chants. Edited by W. A. Muhlenberg, D. D. 37 cts.

The Psalter; or, Psalms of David, &c., &c. Pointed for Chanting. By Robert Janes and James Stimpson. 37 cts.

Canticles; or, the Order of the Daily Service. With the Musical Notation as used in English Cathedrals and Collegiate Churches, together with a Collection of Communion Services, and Chants for the Psalms for the Day and Canticles. $1 00 per dozen.

Deus Misereatur. Being an Adaptation of the Words of Psalm LXVII., with the Gloria Patri, to Music from Zingarelli's celebrated Miserere. 25 cents.

www.ingramcontent.com/pod-product-compliance
Lightning Source LLC
LaVergne TN
LVHW011213110826
845150LV00006B/1421